SEVEN BEHAVIOURS OF SUCCESSFUL RECRUITMENT LEADERS

By Alison Humphries

Contents

Welcome.

Thanks for buying (or borrowing) this book.

This being the case, I'm guessing that you:

Work in the recruitment industry; are an ambitious leader, or aspire to be one; are enthusiastic about professional development, or at least curious.

That's a great start. If these don't all apply to you, I hope you will read on and still get something useful from the book. However, much of what I am going to describe is tricky to implement if you are new to recruitment, a sole trader or not in the industry at all.

And unless you are planning to implement stuff, there's not a lot of point in reading, is there?

Of course, you may have just bought the book to see if it coincides with your own deeply held beliefs. If not, you might just dismiss it as a waste of time. That's how confirmation bias works. All I can say is that if you reject stuff in this book because it's outside your own experience, then you will have missed an opportunity to move out of your comfort zone into the learning zone. And to get there, most people have to go via the "discomfort zone".

One thing I have absolute conviction about is that continuing to learn throughout your career has never been more important than it is now. That's why the chapter "Iterative Improvement" is one of my favourites.

Although this book describes seven behaviours, let me reassure you that this is not just a rework of Stephen Covey's fantastic classic. There has been so much written on the generic subject of leadership, that I need a justification for adding to it.

In homage to Stephen Covey, rather than sneaky imitation, I have grouped my thoughts under the headings of seven behaviours. It's been challenging to group the behaviours of all the good (and not quite as good) leaders I have had the privilege of observing and working with. But without some framework for recall, any book like this can become a series of anecdotes and assertions without a unifying narrative.

Also, I have observed that, across the recruitment industry, there is a tendency to want things applied rather than abstract. Covey's book presents some great principles, but without specific application to the challenges of a recruitment business leader, they can be misinterpreted, or seem very abstract.

So, I want to take the opportunity to talk you through some highly relevant case studies and explain why some "behaviours" may need to be interpreted depending on where you are in the development curve of your business, your market positioning and your culture.

Unsurprisingly, I have made my anecdotes and observations recruitment-specific. Although I do not subscribe to the belief that all recruiters do the same thing, I do believe most recruitment leaders can understand the differences between a temporary and permanent focused business, or between a highly regulated environment, and one that is not, for example. By always giving a level of background, I hope you are able to understand the reasons why I identify some leadership behaviours as strong and others as less strong.

CHAPTER ONE
WHAT IS LEADERSHIP AND WHAT DO WE MEAN BY SUCCESS?

A note on silver bullets

If you are looking for the silver bullet that will transform your business, you may as well put this book down now.

The belief that there is one initiative, one piece of kit, one magic CRM system that will transform your business is particularly stubborn in this industry. Why?

I could speculate about personality types and belief systems, but I think it is simply that the vast majority of recruitment business leaders come from a sales background, are action-orientated and pragmatic. If there is a shortcut, they want to know about it.

This sort of "cognitive miserliness" has been found to attach to people with very high IQs - it's about brain efficiency. But marketing, financial controls, great training and so on are each just one component of a successful recruitment business.

Of course, it suits the suppliers of services to recruitment agencies to play on the silver bullet idea. Just make this one investment, they suggest, and it will transform your business *without you having to change.*

Then again, members of some networking groups pass on similar advice. Often members rush out and copy what someone else has done but no one has considered that lobbing another element into a complex mix of sector, experience, market positioning, skills, and so on won't have the exact same impact as it had elsewhere.

Take M, for example. I became involved with her business because it was struggling, and so was she. She placed staff in healthcare and struggled to make any profit. She was trying to service jobs on frameworks across the whole UK with just three staff. Now, the agreed margins on the frameworks were very small. On top of that, no "transfer" fees were allowed if the client, an NHS Trust, wanted to employ the staff directly, and there were significant requirements for compliance.

M had heard from other healthcare recruiters that they had hundreds of locum staff on assignment and were making a healthy profit. What she hadn't heard from her previous advisor was that the only way you can do this is to have an exceptionally efficient role-fulfilment (job-filling) process.

Instead, M was driving all over the UK to personally undertake face-to-face compliance checks and was working every role that was released under the framework. She hadn't even considered whether there was any flexibility in the bandings assigned to jobs by clients or the expectations of her candidates.

Most of her competitors had created their own efficiencies by:

A. Concentrating on generating qualified candidates for specific trusts

B. Building a relationship with key client personnel so they got advance notice of vacancies

C. Prioritising the redeployment of good locums over trying to submit CVs of unknown candidates to jobs.

Fortunately, I was able to help quickly enough to save the business. But her previous advisors had just recommended increased spending on advertising and marketing. And the additional licences and suppliers they persuaded M to commit to were generating a referral income for those advisors.

What is success?

It's only right to highlight that I have chosen my behaviours based on a particular definition of success.

Many people will be highly successful in their careers, and you have every right to set your own parameters for that. One person wants to create a business that provides a handsome pension, while another wants to turn their business into a social enterprise.

It's also important to recognise the many successful and prosperous sole-trader recruiters who enjoy a great reputation with loyal clients and interesting work.

And those who find that they can make recruitment work around their lifestyle and other interests.

But I had to narrow down my definition of "successful recruitment business leaders" to something we can *all* recognise: those who have created or scaled a business that has a significant capital value which has to be recognised by a substantial business sale or significant growth in profitability, while not depending on the fee generation of just a handful of people.

By some estimates that applies to only about 3% of all recruitment businesses. The market is notoriously fragmented with 80% of UK recruitment businesses employing fewer than 10 people (*source: Recruitment Industry Status Report 2022, REC*), and only 16% of all UK recruitment businesses in existence prior to 2008 (*source: recruitmentbuzz.co.uk*).

So statistically, there are a lot of people out there trying to lead recruitment businesses who have had very little experience of leadership, or insight into what a really large recruitment business looks like. Seeking help to avoid expensive mistakes, accelerate profitable growth and protect your business and reputation should enhance your chances of being in that 3% eventually.

At least that's what my clients (in my NED and board advisory business, Recruitment Leadership Ltd) seem to think. I continue to be blown away by their commitment, entrepreneurialism and willingness to listen to advice.

Exploding one leadership myth

I hope you'll forgive me for killing this myth stone-dead from the get-go. It's the idea that great leadership is different from (or even diametrically opposed to) management.

It goes like this: Leadership is about inspiring, setting a vision and creating an environment where people succeed. While management is all the dull stuff, imposing processes, monitoring, checking on people and implementing. "Managers do things right: leaders do the right thing." Bleurgh!

This is absolute rubbish. The best leaders also manage well.

But I have met hundreds of newish business owners and senior managers who have swallowed this whole. Why not? It's a brilliant excuse to avoid all the grind of actually implementing anything. Or having those "unpleasant" conversations with team members.

Take K, for example. He owned and managed a business placing middle management and operations staff in engineering roles in the Midlands. The business was just about breaking even and employed ten staff altogether - the most they had ever had.

K was vulnerable to staff turnover. So he tolerated very low levels of performance because he did not want to lose people who were billing *something* (average about £6,000 per month per head for those with more than one year of experience). He hoped that they would improve. Each month he was "back on the tools" to make up for a shortfall in revenues.

When I met him, he was determined to move away from personal billing. But he was shy about managing. So, he avoided getting into detail about what his staff were doing. Decisions were taken by referendum (bear in mind that the team had even less experience of running a recruitment business than K did).

It took me one visit, sitting with some individuals at their desks, to work out three specific actions they could take that would significantly improve performance.

The first was so simple, it was embarrassing (for K, not for me).

I found they did no follow-up on placed jobs, or indeed, those that the client had filled via other means. Instead, they were told they needed to do business development, and were chasing advertised jobs and "job leads" picked up from candidates - who had already interviewed for the job. Now, I'm not saying that they should never do this, but that their prioritisation was all wrong.

K agreed to implement this change. But I checked (I'm not shy about that) and I didn't find evidence in a sample of six placed roles.

"I didn't know," K told me, "I can't be everywhere. And they were working from home". K's team knew that K would not check so they were always "going to do it later". He had created an environment where it was assumed that his "processes" were mere suggestions, that his team could take or leave as it suited them.

When we implemented the changes properly (there were several required), K's average revenue went up by more than 100%. More than that, his staff enjoyed better communication with clients and getting recommendations and referrals from placed candidates.

About a year later, having made a profit, we were able to invest in professional marketing to support their efforts. And we got really clear about minimum acceptable performance levels, and processes. Despite his reluctance, K could see that he had to manage people in detail.

If you currently have fewer than 50 staff, there is really no excuse for not getting under the bonnet of your business. Management is essential.

Forming new habits

I think it is really hard to meet all the expectations of a leader these days.

As well as having a vision, you are responsible for implementation. You need to understand accounting, keep tabs on your profitability and forecasts, keep up to date with legislation and compliance, and do this in a volatile, uncertain, complex and ambiguous (VUCA) environment.

Now add in the challenge of managing multiple generations. Many young people now expect their employer to be their social worker, mentor, social conscience, entertainer, financial advisor and inspiration all at once.

And if you offer flexible working, it may feel like you are running two different operating systems (in the office and virtually) at the same time.

Until you get to about 30 staff, it's important to have a good grasp of the technology you are using. And to understand how marketing works. The principles will help you manage people and the business better.

One of my clients, J, a financial recruiter with about 60 staff, had promoted some people to team leader positions for the first time. I ran a management development programme to clarify the expectations and routines we had, and role-played some specific, highly likely scenarios.

J also decided to bring in a speaker who had created an "off the shelf" training module - called "The Listening Leader". J didn't attend himself, but it sounded good and didn't cost much so J thought it would be interesting. But there was no implementation plan. The presenter had no first-hand understanding of the recruitment environment.

Later, one of the newly promoted team leaders had a team member who arrived late for five consecutive days. On the fifth day, the team leader asked why. "My train has been cut by 2 carriages. I can't squeeze on it, so I have to get the later one."

The team member dumped her problem on the team leader. Who listened, then engaged in a lengthy correspondence with the train company in a doomed attempt to get them to reinstate the carriages. Meanwhile, the team member shrugged her shoulders and carried on getting later. And later.

When J found out, he was incredulous. "But I was being a listening leader," pleaded his Team Leader. Yep. For real.

None of us is the finished article. But if you use these seven behaviours as a guide until they become habits, you will definitely increase your chances of success, create clear expectations for your team and more sustainable profit.

Now for the disclaimer:

All the stories and examples are true. However, I have changed the initials of the leaders concerned for a number of reasons.

I have aimed to provide specific examples (without embarrassing the subjects) to illustrate the complexity of a leadership role in modern recruitment companies, no matter how small, or even micro, that organisation is. I find that without context, generalisations about leadership become meaningless. What constitutes great leadership in a military situation under fire is very different from what constitutes great leadership in a research and development team at the cutting edge of science.

I also wanted people to absorb principles, rather than use their attention trying to identify each person and business. But those referred to here will recognise themselves. I wanted to protect confidentiality. Sometimes there were mistakes to be unpicked or false starts that they may not want to see in print.

And please, don't take this book as a suggestion that I myself have always been the perfect role model.

Far from it. Although I describe lots of situations where I was able to make changes that accelerated growth (or avoided damaging or expensive errors), this book is based on observation of all sorts of recruitment business leaders, and working with them over nearly four decades has taught me everything.

I am hugely appreciative of their trust, willingness to take my advice and support with this book. Getting them to their goal faster, and with fewer diversions, has generally turned out to be a good idea!

The book is not a step-by-step, "how to guide", or instruction manual, I'm afraid. *That* book would be too big to digest and it still wouldn't take into account individual circumstances, sectors or goals.

But I hope it will give you some ideas you can implement in your own, unique way, based on a career of working with successful recruitment business leaders.

Postscript:

If you've bought this book, you've probably checked out my credentials on LinkedIn or the Recruitment Leadership website: www.recruitmentleadership.co.uk. So I won't bother explaining them again.

CHAPTER TWO
BEHAVIOUR 1: START WITH THE WHY
(PROBABLY NOT WHAT YOU THINK IT MEANS!)

This chapter is probably not what you think it is.

It's highly likely that you have bought Simon Sinek's excellent book, "Start with Why". However, very few recruitment business leaders that I have met can accurately summarise it. In some cases, they understand it to mean this: from the outset, plan for your business exit. And others may interpret it as meaning: do you have a higher purpose than recruitment? Or merely the pursuit of profit? For example, "to amaze customers", "to make the world a greener place", "to improve careers and businesses", or "to shine a spotlight on our amazing staff".

Let me be clear. I'm absolutely adamant that having a plan is essential. Indeed, there's a whole chapter coming up on that. But trying to build a business based solely on an exit plan tends to result in underinvestment. It makes it hard to build a brand that attracts (and inspires) customers and employees. And remember, you may not be able to control the timing of that exit, due to economic or market changes, personal issues you can't imagine right now, or a business failure, to pick just three possibilities.

I'm also very clear that I would not have spent my entire career in the recruitment industry if I believed it was immoral. Or without social value. Let's never forget that we're dealing with people's work, careers and lives. Finding the right work can be life-changing in every sense, whether that's in a culture in which you flourish, a flexible working model or a series of highly paid contracts with breaks in between. We help people do that, and more.

However, there are now over 40,000 recruitment businesses and agencies registered in the UK alone. In fact, one in every 67 companies registered at Companies House is a recruitment business of one sort or another.

So, before you set up your business, or a new division, or even a new office, I would urge you to revisit "Why".

Why does the world need you to establish another recruitment business?

What can you do better, faster, or cheaper than existing providers?

How will this differentiator benefit your customers? How will the candidate and/or the client experience be improved by your existence? Remember, your clients aren't interested in filling headcount for its own sake.

Think about it. Try and write it down now. What does your business do better, faster or cheaper than the competition?

Statistically, about half of readers' answers will be quite circular, along the lines of: "we will be better because we have a better understanding of the market". What's the matter with this?

1. It's very tricky to sell that proposition to somebody who hasn't already experienced it. If your business is entering the market, and intends to grow its customer base, you and your team will have to do just that. Every day. If your answer is like the one above., you're asking clients and candidates to take that on trust. And with so many recruiters in the market, all claiming something similar, that's quite a big ask.

2. It's completely unsubstantiated. Your assertion that your understanding of the market is better than competitors is entirely subjective. And the minute you hire new staff, your claim is discredited. Because even if *you* have deep and first-hand knowledge of the market you're servicing, not all your staff will.

3. Will this "deep understanding" be demonstrated *every* time a client or candidate uses you? How is it built into your processes? What tools or techniques do you routinely employ? What metrics can you provide to show that your deep understanding will definitely create better outcomes for your customer base? For example, do your placed candidates always stay longer in client companies than the industry average? Are you prepared to put your money where your mouth is in the form of an extended rebate period?

4. How do you know where to find the customers who will value this differentiator? Can you identify them? Can you buy their data? Or is this differentiator merely something that *you* value, that your clients can't see or feel? *And* does it only happen on the good days when they deal with you, not every time?

Now, statistically, another group of readers will have answered with ruthless honesty that they set up their business because they wanted to keep more of the profits than they could as an employee. And hopefully become very wealthy.

If that's the case, the world didn't need your recruitment business. You did. You may be extremely determined, but your "Why" doesn't translate to customers or your future employees.

Or maybe you just hated being someone else's employee. Your boss was greedy, demanding and irrational. So you decided to go it alone. Possibly with an equally disaffected colleague. But I would argue that's not a fully-rounded decision.

In effect, you've decided what you _don't_ want. But not what you want to do and for whom.

Although I spent the first 16 years of my recruitment career in big, listed companies, now, as a NED and advisor, I meet lots of owners of start-ups or micro businesses, because that's the nature of the recruitment industry.

When they get in contact, they are often disillusioned, having failed to grow as quickly as they expected. Or they have realised that they have reached the limit of their own experience and don't know what to do. It may be that they have made some expensive mistakes.

And it's one of the first questions I ask them. Why did the world need you to set up this business? It doesn't have to be a unique service offering, just something that improves on most of the existing provision. One of the things I've noticed is that those who have struggled to grow their business often struggle with this question.
  Take C, for example. C developed his career working in IT recruitment. Although nowadays, that's like saying he recruited "people". So, to be more specific, he focused on Dev Ops contractors in the UK. He had worked at an established brand with around 250 staff.

Through his work, he realised there was a lucrative market that he could move into in Germany. He was also interested in recruiting salespeople for early-stage, high-growth businesses because he had seen the fees that some of his colleagues were invoicing. At the time, salaries in that field were on the increase, and there was plenty of demand.

C was also fed up with his boss. It seemed to him that he was generating all the profits for his boss to enjoy. Meanwhile, he was expected to deliver on his KPIs, attend the office every day and help develop more junior staff.

After a break at Christmas, C decided to hand in his notice. He was confident that he could get around the restrictive clauses in his contract. Therefore he would have an income stream from day one of his new venture.

He also decided to sound out the top biller on the team recruiting sales staff about joining his new venture. The other guy, S, did not work closely with C. But C could see his results in enterprise sales recruitment on the screens around the office. They were good.

S was a little interested. But he decided to leverage C's interest in him by mentioning it to his current boss, thereby alerting the boss to C's departure. So (quite rightly) the boss started monitoring C's emails and made sure he knew which clients he had done business with and could protect those accounts.

When C's approach to S failed, he went to T, who was the second biggest biller on that team. T fancied taking home all the gross profit from his invoicing (who wouldn't?).

They didn't really have time to finesse their plans once the boss had got wind of what was happening. So, together C and T established a brand new business. They registered it at Companies House and named it after themselves.

New recruitment business owners often make this mistake - in fact, more often than not. It makes sense to them at the time. It may even give them a nice warm feeling when they show it to their friends and family.

But it's the number one wasted marketing opportunity. What is it?

They name their new business after themselves.

What's wrong with that, you may ask? Some of our most venerable search firms and recruitment internationals are named after their founders: Michael Page, Robert Half, Robert Walters, Norman Broadbent, and the list goes on. These businesses were established way back in the last century and at the time they wanted - even needed - to sound like the firms of professional advisors (like solicitors and accountants) that they wanted to be. These long-established firms grew and now trade on the wide brand recognition and geographic coverage that was established in the last century.

But businesses starting up today have to establish themselves in the digital world. They need to understand search engine optimisation, market fragmentation and how to communicate a brand in milliseconds. Your business name doesn't have to just "do what it says on the tin" like mine, Recruitment Leadership, but it will be easier to get the attention of your target audience.

And once you have invested thousands in websites, marketing collateral and email campaigns, it's hard to step away from. Because your name, by then, has some brand recognition. *So please don't write to me if you are running a profitable business you have already named after yourself.*

I speak from experience with bad naming choices.

Back in the noughties, I set up my NED/advisory business. There was a fashion at the time for the "Latinisation" of company names. It was an attempt to rebrand and liberate companies from outdated and limiting concepts of what they once were. One of the most memorable was the Post Office Group (Post Office, Royal Mail, Parcelforce) which became Consignia (for a short but expensive period). The name was an expensive disaster and the business back tracked a couple of years later.

Like a lemming, I called my business Amelius Consulting (from the Latin *amelior: to improve or strengthen)*. Clever, huh?

Except that no one searched online for that. No one had enough Latin to recognise the verb. And most people thought my name was Amelia. Some even called me that.

So boy, was I glad (after a spell on a significant change project with a client) to have a chance to rebrand.

I am absolutely not saying that your business will fail if you name it after yourself. But remember that ties you down for the future, your partnership may disintegrate, and - no matter how much your current clients may respect you, you are just not famous enough to rely on your own name to take you to a broader market.

Are you moving away or towards something?

When C and T contacted me, they were in year three and had invoiced about £400,000 to date. It had been much harder than expected to get started because their former boss did enforce the restrictive clauses in their contracts. They had needed to go and find new clients, without an established brand behind them.

They struggled to recruit their own staff successfully. Many of their new starters had actually cost the business money rather than contributed to a profit (this will happen if you lose staff repeatedly in their first year and don't have clear milestones to tell you they are on track - more about this in the chapter "Iterative Improvement").

They were overwhelmed with the day-to-day demands of generating revenue. They had made some mistakes in terms of managing the business. That included forgetting to pay their VAT and PAYE bills. They had also drawn excessive amounts in dividends, resulting in a significant tax liability.

They had both underestimated the amount of work involved in developing a good recruitment business, as opposed to just being good at recruitment.

Having only experienced sales and recruitment, they had underestimated the cost of offices, their tech stack and back office services. And on top of that? There was tension between the two of them. They had very different working styles, and C had no faith in T's sense of urgency or pipeline management.

C was keen to pay for more help. T, who, you will remember, was not the instigator of this business, preferred to keep all profits and saw non-billing staff as nothing but a cost.

So, they had reached an impasse.

I asked them both, without conferring, to complete a short questionnaire prior to our meeting. The very first question on it was: why did you establish your business. The difference between their answers helped to clarify the problem for us all.

C had vague but lofty aspirations. He wanted to be acknowledged as the best recruiter in his specialist markets.

T came at it from a totally different direction. He expected to work hard, sell the business to a larger agency within five years and be able to continue working but without the pressure, remaining in a senior role in someone else's recruitment business.

At this point, they had two resourcers who were being "fed" vacancies and simply found CVs of candidates that C and T often rejected. They could not see a way ahead.

You might reasonably ask why C and T had never discussed the "Why" themselves. Well, when they decided to go it alone, they simply didn't know what they didn't know. Unknown unknowns, if you will.

So, at this point, three years in, they were still introducing themselves to potential clients by saying, "between us, we have 14 years' experience. We just felt that we could do things better than everyone else."

(By the way, that, "14 years' experience" thing, is one of my pet hates. I see it on a lot of recruiters' websites. What it tells me is that you have three people with an average of fewer than five years of experience each. And if all you have done in that five years is the same job in the same market, that's really one year's experience five times over. Plus, the fact that you think that shows deep experience only emphasises to your clients how inexperienced you are. Trust me.)

In the case of C and T, we went back to the first principles.

First, what did they definitely do better than their competitors?

They could find candidates that other recruiters could not. This happened partly through their tech stack and Boolean search skills, and partly because they focused on building networks via referral and recommendation rather than advertising and filtering people only for a specific role.

This "candidate networking" capability was enhanced by narrowing their focus to just three main development platforms, rather than saying yes to every requirement.

Second, on the sales side, T seemed convinced that he was better at identifying talent than other recruiters. He interviewed in detail rather than just relying on CV experience. But he had no evidence. So, next, we started with anecdotal evidence in the form of multiple endorsements. I gave them an action to get a dozen each, featuring these differentiators.

Now, the easiest way to do this is to draft them yourself and send them to your clients to edit (if they wish), then paste them into the LinkedIn request. A recommendation that says "T was really lovely and friendly" doesn't tell other people anything useful. Maybe they won't get along with you. You want it to emphasise what you *do differently and better*, not how nice you are.

The idea is that over time, T and C will be able to collect data and even awards for how their interview-to-offer ratios are better than others, or how much revenue their sales placements have made for their clients.

Third, we needed to make sure that these differentiators were built in. This took some time, but we created templates, processes and KPIs for the resourcers that would eventually turn them into better recruiters. From there, T and C began to feel more confident about letting them talk to clients.

Fourth, we were now able to take a clearer message to potential clients and candidates. On the Dev Ops side, it was something like this:

"Azure Contractors, are you fed up with approaches from recruiters who haven't got the first idea about what you do?"

On the sales side, it was approximately:

"Sales Directors, are you trying to grow quickly to take advantage of your innovative product/service? Do you need to know that your sales team will deliver results for you now by creating their own opportunities? Our methodology probes way beyond CVs".

These messages became central to their brands. They did not sell on speed or price. That was one of their biggest learnings.

If you are going to develop a brand, you need to have a consistent message. And that means saying "no" to some things.

In the early days, they would scrabble around working on any job or client they could find. They worked some "spot" business, and occasionally via a master service provider (MSP) at low margins. They attempted to fill roles in countries and in technologies with which they had no experience.

Now, think about individuals with some of the strongest brands. Maybe you bring to mind Dolly Parton or Richard Branson. Instantly recognisable.

I'm going to pick Bob Ross, the artist who has developed lasting, posthumous fame. His TV series, "The Joy of Painting" was originally screened from 1983 to 1994, which was a success story in itself.

Ross had joined the military in his earlier career and swore when he left that he would never raise his voice again. He also adopted a very distinctive bubble perm hairdo. Whether or not you like his art, he has an amazingly calm presenting style that a lot of people enjoyed in the Covid-induced panic of 2020.

Later, Ross developed cancer. Although he hated it, he maintained his (literally, trademarked) appearance with a wig. Because he knew what his audience expected of the "Bob Ross brand". *You have to make sacrifices to build a brand. And that means saying no to some things, despite the fact that it would be quite convenient to say yes in the here and now.*

Once you have a clear idea of what your brand is - or will be - you can take it to customers who value that. There may be some potential business you don't win because your brand does not click with the audience.

If you are selling Volvos, you don't market speed or sexiness.

If you are selling thorough interviewing and lasting placements, you don't market yourself on price.

Find clients who value the thing you do better than others.

Or to put it another way, don't just think about the Why. Think about the Who as well.

And keep going until you have really maximised your market share before you start to diversify.

Let's develop this idea of clarifying your brand. Here are three movies you may know: The Hangover Part II

Star Wars Episode 1: Phantom Menace
Pirates of the Caribbean: On Stranger Tides.

What have they got in common?

They are movies that were critically and publicly panned at the time but made huge amounts of money nevertheless.

Why? Their producers thought carefully about the Who. This made it easier to promote them.

Think about Netflix. What does the streaming giant know about you?
What actors you like?
What styles you like?
What time of day you log on?
When and where you go on holiday?
Which titles you binge watch and which you abandon (and exactly how far in)?

It's a phenomenal data set. And it allows Netflix to target their advertising very, very well. But it also informs their content development. Because if you know that films featuring action are popular, and so is Keira Knightley, you can put them together and market the result to both groups.

Does that mean I have to stay in my narrow lane of specialism forever?

Categorically, no.

Look at Hays Plc, for example, who expanded from finance recruitment into construction, IT, office support and then across every discipline you can name including a big MSP brand.

But by then Hays was selling on size and reach, not specialism (although consultants there still specialise).

If you didn't do this before you started your business, it's not too late. And it will give your team something to sell that they understand. And for your candidates and clients, something they will value.

Just keep telling people about your Why.

In summary:

- **What do you do better than everyone else?**
- **Can you provide evidence?**
- **How can you make it happen every time?**
- **Can you identify the people who will buy this?**

CHAPTER THREE
BEHAVIOUR 2: LEARN TO BE A BUSINESS PERSON

It is a popular belief that one of the reasons for the (more than) 40,000 recruitment businesses and agencies registered in the UK is the low barriers to entry into the industry.

You can start a business from your bedroom, of course. And you don't need to invest in any stock or machinery up front except a laptop. You can probably get by with just your wits and your networks for a year or so.

But not if you want to grow a business that has capital value.

Even if you have no interest in growing it beyond a lifestyle business, eventually your network of contacts will move on, retire or go elsewhere to another recruiter who can offer a better service because of investment and reach.

Anyway, this line about the "low barriers" to entry is taken on trust. And many new business owners I know only discover what they have missed when they get into deep trouble.

For some time, I advised a business that had established itself in HR recruitment. When a client asked them if they could supply an occupational health worker, they said yes.

What they didn't understand was that they had strayed into the world of "regulated work". They now had a legal obligation (under the Conduct of Employment Agencies and Employment Businesses Regulations 2003) to check that references, qualifications, DBS, training and authorisations were up to date. They just didn't know.

As you can imagine, this backfired spectacularly and cost them a fortune to settle with the client as well as sucking up a huge amount of management time.

The recruitment business owner thought the client should have told him that he had to do this. Well, the information was widely available if he'd looked. But he didn't bother *because it had never been a problem before.*

It's never a problem until it's a problem.

Not being registered with the ICO is not a problem until someone makes a complaint about you.

Not understanding IR35 isn't a problem until HMRC decides to investigate you.

And not knowing that you cannot discriminate against a pregnant woman in recruitment isn't a problem until she decides to bring a claim against you. (Well, actually I think it is.)

The above are all real-life examples that I have encountered in recruitment organisations *in the last 10 years.*

So, this chapter is going to outline some of your obligations as a recruitment business owner. If you thought mastering recruitment in your sector was tricky, fasten your seatbelt. Because you have *a lot more to learn* now that you have set up a business.

And if you have been established for some time, please read this anyway, if only so you can reassure yourself.

Before getting into the weeds on this learning, I'd like to emphasise something really important.

The most successful recruitment business leaders do *not* let this lack of knowledge hold them back. They go ahead anyway.

But what separates them from those less successful is that they learn this stuff rapidly, without losing sight of their main aim, which is to grow the business.

One of my clients, M, is an ambitious and talented recruiter who could produce remarkable revenues himself. From scratch, he generated nearly £400,000 in revenue in his first year.

But M's mistake was that he thought he could copy everything or outsource it cheaply. Without understanding it at all.

So, his terms of business were weak and out of date (copied from a former employer, who had copied them as well).

The marketing agency he paid to build a website and manage his social media ripped him off and didn't finish the website. They had no real experience of recruitment and the need to speak to candidates as well as clients, resulting in the messaging being quite offensive to the candidate pool.

The self-styled "virtual FD" he engaged with did nothing beyond registering the business. He didn't submit the necessary returns, and M was baffled by the technical terms. M was also *embarrassed to say he didn't know things.*

Another business that I worked with (in a regulated sector) supplied hundreds of staff via MSPs to local authorities across the country. They assured me that their compliance was outstandingly good. The MSPs audited them regularly, sampling candidate files for completeness and quality. They had a string of good passes.

But their compliance only covered those audits. So when we got a call from a manager in one of the end-user clients, saying that one of her staff had been harassed about a reference by one of our contractors, it unearthed a big-scale problem.

You see, on establishing references for new contractors, these consultants had been telling the contractor if it wasn't good enough - indeed, sending them a copy of the reference - and advising them to go back to the referee and get it changed. Not once, but hundreds of times.

(There are circumstances when people can access a reference about themselves, but the starting position is that it is confidential between the person who gives it and the person who requests it.)

You see, it's never a problem until it's a problem. In this case, the end-user client hiring manager was protecting a member of her staff who had been threatened and harassed by the contractor and wanted us sacked by the MSP, which would have cost us just shy of a million pounds in revenue.

And there's more. I was working with one business which had grown rapidly but the founders were the only people who had experience of recruitment from anywhere else. They had never looked closely at what their new staff were doing. *Which included sending out CVs with candidate contact details all over them.*

Yes, really. No one had ever told these people that this was a bad idea. Not just for commercial reasons (the amount of lost revenue makes me sad) but because this was clearly a data breach. A candidate can reasonably believe that his/her private contact details would not be shared with a potential employer without express permission.

How did I find this out when their bosses (the founders, who did have recruitment experience gained elsewhere) had not? The answer is I no longer take stuff for granted. **I ask people not just to "tell me" but also to "show me".**

On the "new client" questionnaire I use when a recruitment business wants to engage my services as a NED/Advisor, one of the questions is:

Compliance: on a scale of 1 to 10 (where 10 equals very confident), how confident are you about compliance with the Conduct Regs, IR35, KIDs, Immigration and

Asylum, DPA, GLAA, GDPR, AWR, NMW, Equality Act? Do you have a staff handbook?

The most worrying answer is 10. Because if compliance isn't a worry, then the business is almost certainly unaware of the risks they face.

So, now to give you some guidance.

1. When you register the business at Companies House, understand the duties and liabilities of a Director. If you are going into business with a partner, get a Shareholders Agreement drawn up by a lawyer. Make sure you understand whatever compliance your market requires.

You and your new business partner are probably the best of friends right now, but things can change drastically. I worked with two businesses which almost entirely collapsed because the founding partners suddenly wanted completely different things.

In one case, one partner reacted to a sudden shift in the market by wanting to shut up shop. He had heard that even small recruitment business owners sell for a multiple of five times EBIT, and he didn't want to hang around for what he thought would be a much-reduced EBIT after Covid. But this idea of his wealth was based on selling the business as a thriving going concern in a trade sale (that doesn't apply when the market is in a downturn and the partnership has disintegrated).

There was no Shareholders Agreement in place. When his business partner thought they could survive, the first partner assumed he could live off the £800,000 he thought his business partner would somehow pay him to exit. No one had explained to him that, with no agreed plan for separation and no agreed means of valuation, his departure would be compensated as a basic division of assets. A *lot* less than he thought. It was a financially, legally and emotionally draining time. Like a really acrimonious divorce.

In another case, one business partner was married and had children while the other remained single and very focused on work. The first wanted to take all the profit out of the business in dividends each year, leaving no reserves for a downturn, investment or new hires.

Even a start-up business needs a minimum of three months of overhead in reserve. Taking out all the profits and treating the business like your own personal piggy bank is going to get you into trouble. *It is, legally, a separate entity from you.*

2. Learn to speak accounting.

This is one that some recruitment business owners have a very fixed mindset about. "I just don't get it - can't I leave that to my accountants?"

The answer is no. Your firm of chartered accountants has to follow a reporting format dictated by HMRC. Not you. So *you* need to be clear about what *you* need in terms of management information.

And (although many of them think they can), I have never found a firm of Chartered Accountants who offer good business advice to a micro recruitment business. Tax advice, yes. Balance sheet, yes.

B ran a finance recruitment agency placing staff in permanent positions. He had 15 staff when I became involved in the business. I recommended that we needed to build a contract division to create some long-term visibility of income, and thereby enhance the value of the business in the long term.

Now, if you have tried to do this, you'll know that it's not going to make a massive profit in the early stages. His accountant told him he was mad to do it. The same accountant also told him to withdraw all the profits as dividends - without checking that all VAT and PAYE had been paid. So B emptied the bank account. Big mistake.

(Afterwards, he followed my advice on contract instead, and now has 30 staff generating three times as much profit. Plus he can sleep at night because of the future income from contracting.)

My point is that, if you don't bother to learn the language of accounting, and carefully interrogate it, you are very vulnerable to bad advice. Or even fraud.

I hope you already know this. But just in case:

A. Understand the difference between capital expenditure items (balance sheet) and sales and overheads (Profit & Loss). One client thought he was making a modest profit because it appeared on his P&L each month. But because his business loan, agreed payments to a former business partner and car payments were actually on his balance sheet, he was in fact running at a loss. Next stop: cash flow problems.

B. Get everyone (yourself, your staff and your accountant) to use the same terms and definitions for revenue, cost of sale, net fee income, operating profit and profit after tax.

C. Get a monthly P&L report based on sales invoiced, not deals agreed. Include overheads which are invoiced in that month, not just what's paid out of the bank account.

D. After a year of trading, create a budget for the next year, and every year after that. It doesn't run the business for you, but it will provide a plan and some insight into what investment is affordable and when. Remember businesses have bad months. Make your expectations realistic.

E. Manage your sales staff by focusing on sales made. Manage the business by sales invoiced (which is when an accountant recognises them). And always check the cash that comes in. If there's a pattern of a drop-off between these three (at an individual or company-wide level) then you need better processes.

F. Build up reserves. Don't treat every personal best as an excuse for a great big party. (I knew a business in marketing recruitment with ten staff that beat its own monthly record by £3000 one month. They then spent the £3000 on a party. That was before paying out the commission due, so they actually made *less* profit that month.)

G. As a business owner, be prepared not to be the highest-paid person in the business sometimes. Your reward really comes later.

3. Look at your business for efficiencies.

If you were running a manufacturing business, you'd try to minimise wastage and "non-compliant product". You'd probably study your production line to see how it could produce more, or operate more efficiently. And you'd review suppliers of raw materials all the time.

I worked with a business operating in the facilities management sector. They had been in business for over 10 years but profits had been flatlining for some time.

They had good relationships with some major accounts. But over two years, their average fee had declined and they weren't making any additional placements. As the market tightened and became more candidate-driven, they placed more and more adverts (at an increasing cost) without looking at the effectiveness of the ads. On top of that, staff always went along with the terms that had been put in place with clients three years ago.

By sampling, we found that 50% of the CVs his team had paid to download from job boards were already on the CRM.

When we did the analysis, they were also taking longer to fill jobs. In fact, the time from instruction to agreed start had increased from 27 to 56 days. That wasn't just a month of waiting patiently to issue an invoice. It was a month spent finding more candidates for the clients who still expected a beauty parade. More time keeping candidates warm in case the offered candidate dropped out. And more time, in effect, helping clients refine their specifications by trial and error.

It wasn't just a question of us recognising these inefficiencies. We had to come up with an action plan to fix them. This is not the same as just telling people (see chapter "Have a Plan"). This included using the "waste product" of candidates rejected for a specific role. These became candidates that could be marketed, and because we kept in touch, they sometimes filled jobs really quickly.

But the biggest thing we were struggling with was the mindset of the staff. In a client-led market, they accepted that the client was king. They hadn't changed their behaviours even though the market conditions were reversed.

The biggest drag on your business growth is the pull of the status quo. If the status quo is generating a *little* success, that's an even bigger force acting against change and improvement.

So, a business where people are taking home *some* commission for generating very moderate fees will need a serious, thorough plan to achieve a real step up. This leads me to...

4. Targets, expectations and minimum standards.

I've met with a lot of business owners who use the term "target" indiscriminately. Often what they are describing is a barely acceptable minimum.

It's really important to get this straight in your own head, so you are giving clear and consistent messaging to your team.

Minimum standards are standard for the grade. There should be minimum fee generation standards written down for each grade of consultant, and minimum KPIs to ensure a pipeline. Spell them out and be sure to take formal action, promptly and consistently, if anyone doesn't meet them. The aim of this is remedial and diagnostic. Not to push someone out. But unless you apply the procedure consistently, you expose yourself to the risk of discrimination claims, and the perception of bias or favouritism.

Expectations should be spelt out, ideally in a career planner. It may be that senior consultants are expected to generate £15,000 per month, but the minimum standard is £10,000 when averaged over 2 months. You will be using expectations in your budget.

A new joiner will take some time to ramp up as they build their networks. You can clarify expectations in terms of vacancies generated, interviews arranged, and contractor bookings during this period. But act quickly when someone is not on track, even if they have managed to pull in a deal. Yes, people do sometimes get lucky early, and we tend to assume that they know what they are doing. Six months later, no further revenues.

Targets are personal and developmental. A target may be to meet the criteria for promotion. Or to win a major account. Or to improve offer-to-acceptance ratios. It needs to be agreed between the individual and their manager to have any impact. Achieving a target requires recognition, financially or otherwise.

5. Manage suppliers by understanding what they do.

I have often met business owners, many of whom have extensive experience as recruiters, who saw marketing as some sort of frilly extra. There are far fewer of these now, but they thought of marketing largely as vague PR, insignificant compared to their own sales efforts.

The same business owners often told me they were leaving all their content creation to an agency. Or a 22-year-old "first-jobber" in the corner who "totally gets social media".

Whether you hire internally or use an external company, you need to understand what you are aiming to achieve for the business. For most, marketing aims it boil down to more, relevant candidates registering and more, relevant clients engaging you.

Marketing is part of that mix. Indeed, when a recruitment consultant tells me that a job or candidate "just phoned in", it has usually been prompted by marketing.

But the effects of marketing are cumulative. So, if your salesforce continues to do the same things, you will want to see that your key statistics are improving with your investment in marketing (website visits, downloads etc), which should indicate future gains in candidates and clients and therefore a more productive salesforce.

Yet very few business owners measure this data regularly. If you only look at it irregularly, there will always be speculation. "That mail-out probably got no response because it went out during the World Cup", or "that advert may have been ineffective because a lot of people were on holiday".

Speculative rationalisation butters no parsnips for me. What I want to know is what your marketing will do differently to increase our traffic.

Also, it's a very rare first-jobber who can produce industry-specific content that establishes you as a leading-edge thinker in your sector. Please don't just post for the sake of it. And keep your "behind the scenes" posts to 20%. You may be getting lots of engagement, but it's all from your mates and colleagues, not from your target market.

Now, I've picked on marketing but you need to think about what you want to achieve from all your suppliers.

If you are investing in a new CRM, what is the expected ROI? Is it to reduce job-board spending by having a more searchable candidate list? Is it to generate better prompts to action, by diarising key follow-ups and contact points for the recruiter? If it is better management information, what are you going to do with it?

6. If you want to grow a valuable business, be prepared to make some tough decisions.

It's very important to make your peace with not being the most popular person in your business at all times.

Over-rewarding staff is a common issue. I routinely look at the pay-out ratio in businesses I work with. You calculate it like this:

(Salaries + commissions + employer's pension contributions + employer's NICs + cost of any other direct benefits) x 100 ÷ total net fee income.

This percentage has been steadily growing across the recruitment industry for many years. In 2014 it was 20% for contract/temp businesses and 26% for permanent businesses.

By 2017, it had increased to 32% and 40% respectively (*source: APSCo Deloitte Recruitment Index*).

Check yours, please. And if it's much over 40% make a plan to improve productivity, bring down fixed costs or both. You may need to defer some hiring until you have done so.

Remember, a commission scheme is not forever. I would review it every year (make sure your policy says so, and it is not a contractual right). Because commission needs to incentivise the behaviours that drive *future* success.

7. Don't just copy terms, employment contracts and policies from your old employer.

I have yet to find a business where I couldn't improve one or more of these because times change. New issues occur. Case law interpretations change.

One client lost a number of his trained consultants to clients, who hired them to create in-house talent acquisition teams. I inserted a clause in his terms that said they could not solicit staff, and if one applied to them, the fee would be calculated on the whole P60 earnings against that person's name.

The fact that a client called him immediately to object to this clause told him everything. Yes, the client acknowledged, pinching staff from good recruiters was part of *his* talent acquisition strategy.

Here's another: I regularly come across staff handbooks that are nothing but "off the shelf" box-ticking exercises issued by "HR agencies". Most of the policies simply say "it is our policy to obey the law" or "to act reasonably". These are not doing any management heavy lifting for you, and are usually inadequate.

Please, keep up to date with all the relevant laws and regulations.

Read the reports and data issued by reputable sources like the REC, APSCo, lawyers and accountants. There will be more on this in the chapter "Iterative Improvement".

Finally, like any business leader, you need to get in control of your lifestyle.

What used to be forgiven when you were an employee, will be remembered now you are boss.

But the day when you know everything will never come. Whether it's a new business or a new division, **don't let it stop you from making a start.**

In summary:
- **Understand accounting and reporting**
- **Manage suppliers effectively**
- **Get more efficient**
- **Stay up to date**
- **Clarify expectations, targets and performance minimums.**

CHAPTER FOUR
BEHAVIOUR 3: FOCUS ON THE COMMUNITY

This is not a chapter about your corporate social responsibilities.

By now I hope you have several points you want to review or implement in your business.

Even if you are confident that you do everything in the last two chapters, it makes sense to check in with your team to see whether they have a clear idea of your "Why", and whether the processes that underpin it are in use consistently.

This chapter is going to take a slightly different turn. And please forgive me for squeezing four points into one chapter, which some may say should be split over several.

Focusing on *your community* is about the way you treat the people that make it up. And *your community* breaks down (broadly) into four groups:

A. Colleagues
B. Clients
C. Candidates
D. Wider environment

Let's take colleagues first. One of my observations about the most successful leaders in the industry is that they are *consistently courteous* to their own staff and keep them engaged through communication.

That doesn't mean that they bend over for them or shy away from challenging them. They are clear about expectations and behaviours and they act promptly when someone is out of line. There's a lot more on this in the chapter "Start from Strong Roots".

But they don't swear *at* them or lose their temper easily. They don't panic. And they don't lie about important stuff. On top of that, they always put effort into getting people onside.

Many readers will, unfortunately, have had experience working for bosses who are the opposite. I know I did. And that behaviour is infectious. Those who feel under constant threat often do the same to others. Or they just leave.

During the first phase of the Covid pandemic, a lot of people realised their boss's true colours. Some bosses panicked and even pushed their staff to work while claiming furlough money (so I'm told).

Nobody knew how things were going to pan out, or how long the crisis would last. But those who have gone on to achieve the highest levels of success since are those who were prepared to say what they could and couldn't do and didn't load their own anxieties onto others.

J is a shining example of this. At his professional services recruitment consultancy, he is always courteous to staff and makes time to talk to everyone, acknowledging every success. This includes business support staff and suppliers. So, he had a lot of "community credit" in the bank.

Although a few powerful suppliers took the view that they were going to demand regular payments even if it put J out of business, most of his suppliers agreed to a break in payments and he kept in touch with them to be clear about when he could "switch them on again".

But J and I had developed a crisis plan. We'd done it in the years of plenty (well, 2019) when everything was looking rosy because it was easy to talk about when we were feeling confident.

Then, no one could have known the exact shape the next crisis (Covid) would take, but what we could do was identify certain thresholds in a hypothetical crisis, and the actions we would take if the business hit them. They were:

- A 20% decline in net fee income over two successive months
- A 50% decline in fillable jobs over two successive months
- A drop-off of new starters on contracts to zero in any one month (he only had 15 at the start of the pandemic, being new to the temp/contract market)
- A decline in average margin of more than 30% per deal that isn't due to an anomaly, like a substantial exclusive arrangement
- If net profit fell below X for three successive months.

As you can imagine, the actions included freezing internal recruitment, accelerating terminations of probationers and reducing advertising and incentive spending.

Then there were more serious steps to be taken if the situation worsened. These included reducing office space and asking staff to take a voluntary, temporary pay cut.

And they did. Because the plan was written down, logical and communicated at a time when we weren't in a crisis. The team knew that this was a carefully considered plan and it wasn't a sneaky attempt to feather J's own nest. Indeed, he took an even bigger pay cut. But the business steadied rapidly, the team trusted J and their pay was restored at the earliest opportunity. And he kept communicating with everyone throughout.

J has one of the most successful internal talent acquisition processes I know. He recruits both trainees and experienced hires because he has a very strong employer brand, but also because he is well known in the recruitment community. He doesn't offer the highest basic salaries, and billing expectations are higher than most comparable businesses. But he plays a long game.

Many of the experienced hires he has made are referrals from other staff he has hired, or even from clients who have used them.

And almost all of the experienced ones are people he has been communicating with for nine months or longer.

When they come for an interview, J invites them to speak to his staff about the company culture and benefits etc. They do, but what they also *always* talk about is J's calm, focused and courteous leadership.

Engagement

An awful lot has been written and said about staff engagement and I don't intend to repeat it here. But I do want to emphasise that **engagement does not mean throwing benefits at your staff.**

I knew a leader who actually gave someone the task to produce a monthly report on what benefits other recruiters were offering. He intended to match them in an attempt to become the most attractive recruitment employer in the city. What he didn't do was ask for a detailed breakdown.

So he heard that X was offering a higher percentage in commission, but what he didn't hear was that they pay much lower basic salaries.

He heard that Y had increased annual leave, but what he didn't hear was that they had invested nothing in training.

This leader had confused employee happiness with employee engagement. And it cost him a fortune, without generating any increase in productivity. Nobody turned down the extra benefits, naturally.

Employee engagement is the connection employees feel with the mission, vision and values of a business. It is the sense of playing an important role in the pursuit of a worthy goal, and being recognised fairly for that.

It was originally "measured" by total discretionary effort - the amount of additional, unpaid work and thought that employees put in above contracted minimums. That measure has dropped out of sight now, but the focus of successful leaders on their colleague community is absolutely critical to it.

The Client Community

When I worked at Hays Plc, the career path for managers was designed to take them away from the front line as soon as possible. And as they moved up the hierarchy, clients became even more remote. That may have been what contributed to the impression of a high staff turnover.

Back then it wasn't quite the vast organisation it is today. (Originally, Hays was a shipping and chemicals company until it acquired Accountancy Personnel, and later divested all its heavy industrial business to become a recruitment giant. That's why there is a Hays Wharf on the Thames in London).

So, the managers' understanding of the market, what worked and what to focus on became quite second-hand. The difficulty with this is that they then became pretty reliant on "filtered" information from their subordinates. So if a front-line consultant told them that the market was slow or there was downward pressure on fees in their area, for example, they didn't have anything else to go on.

Now, I don't want to impugn the entire staff of Hays in the 1980s and 1990s. But it did become clear to me that the best people were often removed from the customer interface and replaced with beginners.

And, as inexperienced managers, they banged on and on about KPIs - but quantity only.

Now there are three aspects of individual inputs that can impact outputs in recruitment. Let's leave external market forces and brand recognition out of this for now (as they aren't in the control of individual recruiters).

They are:

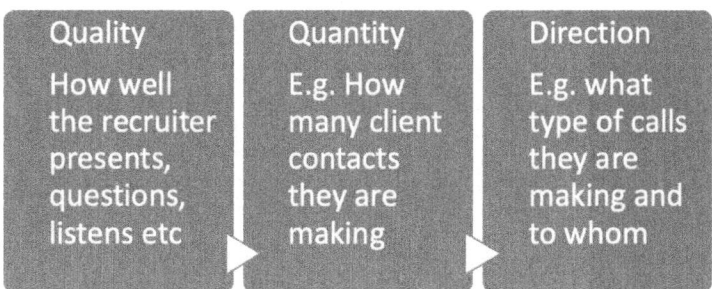

If you focus solely on quantity, because you are so far removed from clients that you can't judge the quality and direction of efforts, you just get a lot of poor contacts.

Ironically, that might even be *damaging* your brand - but with lots of clients!

Ever since, I have tried to maintain *some* personal interaction with the client base. That way I have some interesting conversations, which in turn inform how I manage the business. It gives me ideas that simply would not have come otherwise. Like establishing several "statement of works" businesses that went on to generate millions of pounds of profit, in three different companies.

Or offering training in addition to recruitment services, which then generated more recruitment business. But more of that later in the "Be Agile" chapter.

It's important to be visible in key accounts.

If a client is giving you repeat business - even if that client is a master service provider - your face as a business leader at meetings tells them that you value their business. You can't do it for every client, but at least your top ten should ideally get a visit once a year.

I advised R to do this in his business supplying temporary and contract staff in renewable energy. He was reluctant at first because he thought it would raise expectations that he would be servicing their vacancies personally. Also, two of the top ten clients were based in the Middle East and Singapore.

So, I worked with him to focus his questions differently. He still took the recruiter who managed the account day-to-day with him. But instead of just asking about jobs, we focused on him asking about business. He learned multiple things via this process:

1. That clients have their own KPIs, and just filling empty seats is not one of them. In fact, if they could achieve their business objectives without hiring, then they certainly would.

2. That clients are interested in how their recruitment outcomes compare with their competitors - using proper data and reports, rather than a recruiter just asking, "could you pay a bit more?" They listened carefully to his recommendations on shortening the selection process and improving their induction process.

3. That if you don't ask about the client's impressions of your service, misinformation can take hold (one client had got mixed up about who had provided two contractors who got into a fight and stabbed each other).

4. If you always leave the frontline recruiter to sort out problems, you may miss an opportunity to fix a larger problem. In this case, the client noticed that our contractors were grumbling about how long it took to get their expenses refunded. The recruiter on the front line had always had to do workarounds to fix individual cases, but R saw that it was a pattern and was able to change the whole process at our end.

5. If you raise the conversation from "jobs" to "business", you can get an early heads-up on new projects.

As a direct result of one client meeting, R went on to make a proactive proposal to staff a new site as master service provider. It didn't go out to tender, or to some bigger businesses. That contract generated £400,000 in net profit in year one.

The Candidate Community

It's certainly true to say that there has been a real shift in the balance of power between candidates and employers over the last few years.

According to the Chartered Institute of Personnel and Development, 94% of HR managers have been "ghosted" by candidates to whom they have offered a job.

There won't be many readers who have not had to manage candidates who drop out of the process, accept counter-offers or reject offers because they have several better ones.

So, it makes sense that leaders have some communication with their candidate community. At least the ones you have placed.

Many years ago, working in a 90% temp business, I introduced net promoter scoring (NPS). The concept was still in its infancy in recruitment then. A, the recruitment business owner, showed considerable reluctance to implement this as he thought it would show that the most productive staff did not always give a great service to their temps and candidates.

We circulated the simple survey (initially just to placed contractors and later to all those who had interviewed with our clients). We were able to see results segmented by individual recruiters. And they showed that A had been significantly wrong in his assumption.

The most productive recruiters had the highest NPS scores. They were productive precisely because they could redeploy their workers, and in some cases get them to agree to "help the recruiter out" by covering a job that was at a lower grade than usual, in the short term.

But the other thing it clearly showed was that, in cases where a low NPS had been given, 50% of those scores were not as a result of the recruiter, but the compliance and payroll staff. Now, these staff regarded any request or feedback from temps as a nuisance. One had even said to a temp, "if you would stop phoning me, I might have processed your pay by now! But now it's going to the bottom of the pile. You were late submitting your timesheet."

Now, A would never have become aware of this without some communication with the candidate community. It didn't have to be face-to-face. But that led to some major changes in customer service orientation and running payroll twice a week at least.

And the impact of those changes showed up later in the redeployment and retention of workers, and the recommendations they made to others.

Wider Community

This varies significantly between sectors, but being visible with the professional associations of which your clients are members has been a really great investment for some of the most successful leaders.

This doesn't mean just sponsoring awards or pitching a stand at their conferences. Those are transactions and you must decide whether the R.O.I. is justified.

Successful leaders make sure they are integrated with these communities.

Helping, not selling.

A, in the example above, was persuaded to attend regional members' meetings. He made the mistake of being in full sales mode at first. Hand outstretched, he scattered his business cards like confetti, asking people to remember him when they were hiring.

The results were zero. But I persuaded him to try again. The analogy I used was this:

If you were looking for a romantic partner you probably wouldn't go to a bar and approach a stranger saying, "Hey! Do you want to hear all about me? Get a load of my physique, my stuffed wallet and what former partners have said about me!"

No, you'd approach someone you liked the look of by noticing something about them. You'd ask them about themselves, maybe try to find something you have in common. If they are responsive, you might suggest a follow-up meeting, where you can show you've been thinking about what they said.

So, A went back to the regional meetings. He listened to the talk and asked people about their businesses. Sure enough, he identified some potential new business. But he held back from swooping on it with figurative £ signs in his eyes. Instead, he called the next day to say that he's been thinking about what they had said and he thought he may have a solution. Were they open to a meeting?

A went on to generate quite a lot of referred business from that network. And most of it was senior retained perm, taking his business into a very successful new market.

Another example is Corporate Social Responsibility (CSR) - and there's no doubt it has risen up the agenda dramatically. But people can spot "greenwashing" and lip service a mile off.

D was the MD of an established business with 70 staff. He had no personal interest in CSR but felt that there was a marketing opportunity being missed. He set out with the aim of generating lots of "behind the scenes" posts that said how much money his business had raised for charity.

He delegated responsibility for this to the marketing team. Relatively inexperienced, they approached it rather like those "wear your own clothes days" that you may remember from school. They googled fundraising and awareness days and then arranged some random "fun" way of recognising it that would generate small donations from their own staff.

Causes included everything from Children in Need to Movember.

They generated very small amounts and became a distraction from work. Many employees felt strongly that they wanted to do something meaningful, for a cause they cared about.

So D made a shortlist of charities nominated by individuals and picked a couple himself. He announced that they would support a different charity each quarter. But there was very limited support. The charities were of "personal interest" to individuals only.

Finally, D was persuaded to offer all staff one day a year to actually do work for a good cause. Organising this took some time, but the staff volunteered to provide CV and interview advice to a group of disadvantaged people via a registered charity. They were doing something worthwhile in the community, and D decided to give the equivalent of half of their salaries on those days to the charity.

There are lots of ways you can engage with the community. Professional associations like the REC, regional business associations, sector bodies, public sector organisations like growth hubs, charities, and the list goes on. But make it an authentic, long-term commitment.

Take L, for example; he set up his own industry networking group and raises money through dinners in aid of his cause. He calculates that it has repaid his investment many times over in referrals.

In summary:
- **Communicate calmly, courteously and consistently**

- **Be visible to your key stakeholder groups**
- **Help, not sell**

CHAPTER FIVE
BEHAVIOUR 4: ITERATIVE IMPROVEMENT

BUSINESSILLUSTRATOR.COM

Sharp-eyed readers will have noticed that many of the examples and anecdotes I have used about recruitment business leaders are really focused on things they got wrong, not what they habitually did right to be successful.

There are a few reasons I've done this:

A. Frankly, they make more interesting stories than, "B was totally marvellous and never put a foot wrong". And yes, lots of us find it reassuring to think, "I would have handled that better" or even, "I would never have done that".

B. Explaining the consequences of a leader's misstep is more likely to motivate you to act than outlining the benefits of avoiding pain. No matter how forward-looking we like to think we are, present pain is a more powerful motivator than potential future gain. I hope I've addressed this in the chapter "Be a Business Person" and there is more coming.

C. This is the most important one. **I want to show you that those who build or scale really impressive, successful recruitment businesses are never the finished article. But what they habitually do is look to improve.**

Whenever recruitment business leaders (let's call them RBLs know we've got to know each other) get in touch with me to discuss my work as a NED and Board Advisor, I already know that they have a strong drive to improve. And it takes some guts to say this after those RBLs have been leading people for some years.

But you'll remember (I hope!) what I said in "Learn to be a Business Person":

The biggest drag on your business growth is the pull of the status quo. If the status quo is generating a *little* success, that's an even bigger force acting against change and improvement.

So, the most successful RBLs are never complacent.

But still, I do meet some people who really want more success, but don't want to make the changes that are necessary to scale their business. For example, they really don't want to employ an operations manager because it means lower dividends.

Or they just don't want to manage staff and think that maybe I'll do that for them.

Or they refuse to follow any processes, thereby making it impossible for people to work with them (ask many accountants in the industry).

The most successful RBLs are always looking for ways to improve.

I had this quote on my business cards from my first day as a NED - it's usually attributed to Abraham Lincoln: "Give me six hours to chop down a tree and I'll spend the first four sharpening the axe."

The focus is on planning, preparation and thought before taking action.

So, the first point I want to cover is the need to seek expert advice with an open mind.

Some of you may detect some self-interest here, so I'm going to cover this first to get it out of the way before getting into the meatiest part of this chapter.

Choosing the right expert advice is hard. There are a lot of people out there offering it, many based on surprisingly limited experience.

If you are hiring a NED or an accountant, make sure they have experience of recruitment. Otherwise, you'll be paying someone while *you* explain things to *them*.

Don't confuse trainers with real business advisors. There are some very effective trainers out there, but if they haven't run several businesses, they won't understand how all the functions interact. So, they will focus on developing skills (if you're lucky) when you need to change your reward system, CRM, marketing, KPIs or management as well to get the change you seek.

Next, suppliers often have a very good understanding of the issues their customers face. But they are in the business of selling a product, or a membership subscription where the members provide the content. They will make their money through licensing, membership fees or referral fees. They will not get down in the weeds with your business or make sure that the implementation happens and the system is used.

Now for the third group of advisors. Ambitious RBLs are often dazzled by wealth. I get this - they see people who have made millions in a business exit and they expect that those people are geniuses. Their glamour is inspirational. Their success is, surely, proof that they can help you.

Maybe. But when you look at it, many such people got successful in businesses that were already successful. And they weren't very hands-on even at the time they exited. So, they have no experience of recruiting in the digital age, and with a largely

Generation Z workforce. And they may only have worked in one business or sector, so are in no position to assess what might work in yours.

Now, back to *your* business.

Have you heard the old chestnut, "culture eats strategy for breakfast"?

The late, brilliant Consultant and Writer, Peter Drucker, meant that **no matter how well-designed your strategic plan is, it will fall flat unless your team shares the appropriate culture.** At the end of the day, the people who implement the plan matter.

It's important to clarify that he *didn't* mean that strategy was unimportant, but, to me, **culture is closely entwined with your own hiring and your own learning and development. They all interact with each other.**

Take R, for example. He was a very driven individual with a strong work ethic, a sharp brain, and he was a professional athlete until an injury forced early retirement. At this point, he had turned his hand to recruitment and achieved considerable success with the same discipline and focus. After reaching board level, he established his own business.

R wanted to scale up rapidly. He wanted a culture that reflected his own self-reliance, focus and goal orientation. So, he set about recruiting people like him. People with good degrees and a history of sporting achievement.

But it was hit-and-miss. Staff recruitment and turnover became a problem and so the business plateaued.

R was hiring the wrong people. He hired for external (CV) attributes instead of identifying *aptitudes*, like drive, goal orientation and self-improvement.

I frequently discover that recruiters are quite bad at interviewing for aptitudes and behaviours. When I show them how to question to gain evidence of aptitudes, they often realise it is a benefit to their external recruitment activity for clients as well.

So, when a client says that they want to recruit "an engineer with strong communication skills" ask them how they identify those skills in their current team. Push them to describe what specific behaviours they observe. Because if your client wants someone who writes detailed, precise memos with perfect grammar, and you think you're hiring someone who is charismatic and good at public speaking, someone is going to be disappointed.

Back to culture. The people you hire will inform the culture and, as a micro-business, they will take their lead from you. Remember that cultures vary quite a lot - especially between entrepreneurial start-ups and more mature businesses. You probably know people who have tried to make that switch and failed.

It's important for business owners to recognise that the culture and hiring that make for success at the start-up stage are rarely required in a more mature organisation.

Let's think about the development of a business organisation in phases. Start-up, growth, maturity, renewal.

In recruitment at least, start-ups are almost always owner-managed and everyone does everything. It can be exhilarating; people feel evangelical about their brand and the focus is on getting the word out. There are few (or no) controls other than what the founder decides.

In the growth phase, organisations start hiring and dividing up responsibilities. More processes have to be followed and responsibilities delegated. In recruitment, this might be when you hire an operations manager. Managing cash becomes important.

I think there is also a second part of the growth phase. This is critical to scaling. It's when you have data to manage your business and some idea of what works so can replicate it (for example, via L&D). On the sales side, you will need to develop a management infrastructure. Good RBLs will be a little more externally facing at this stage, looking at what is going on outside their businesses.

A tiny percentage of recruitment organisations reach what most business commentators would call maturity. A mature recruitment business will have strong and reliable cash flow, visibility of future revenues and succession plans. They will be aiming to build market share, or maybe expand to new territories.

After that, renewal. Because the world outside doesn't stand still. And the alternative is decline.

It doesn't take a genius to see that culture will (have to) change as the business develops. That doesn't mean that you can no longer hire driven, goal-orientated salespeople. Steve Jobs (famously always sharpening the saw) created his Skunk Works at Apple for innovation. It was allowed to operate under completely different principles, and a culture different from the rest of Apple.

Back to *your* business.

If you are going to lead it forward, you need to get your metaphorical periscope up soon after start-up.

There are myriad ways you can do this. Listen to podcasts, read the trade press, attend conferences and talk to your peers as well as customers.

You may well encounter facts and data that don't align with your own experience. It's human nature to be sceptical when presented with data that runs counter to what you know. We question the source, the motives of the source and the sample group.

V founded and ran an agency placing permanent professionals in the marketing world. The team had struggled to hire but prided itself on its client relationships. It was especially strong in the creative sphere, as well as account managers in the marketing agency sector. Occasionally they hired for a corporate on the back of an agency referral, or when a client had gone in-house.

However, marketing agencies were on the wane. More and more businesses started to realise they needed to build their own internal marketing capability, and increasingly what they were looking for was digital expertise and data analytics. They also began to recruit staff on a project-by-project basis.

V didn't see it coming because he was experiencing a steady demand from his marketing agency clients for replacement staff. If he had been a little more on the front foot with this, networking and looking at trade news, he might not have lost quite so much market share to much newer competitors. The business went from a profit of £2,000,000 to a profit of £400,000 in four years.

When he was shown data, he was sceptical. He thought of a temporary contract business as a lot of hassle and was alarmed about the administration.

At the same time, his pay-out ratio to his staff (see "Learn to be a Business Person") was dangerously out of control. Because he had kept his well-rewarded staff without any clear expectations of productivity, it was almost impossible to extricate himself.

So, periscope up.

A final point on internal recruitment

If you are ever going to be able to delegate some or all of your internal hiring, you need to be able to explain what you are looking for. So, clear definitions of aptitudes.

You need to make sure that everyone understands the standards you expect. So, if the only evidence someone can present of, say, their money motivation is that they did a supervised stint at university calling alumnae for donations, it wouldn't be strong enough for me. I might be interested if they had brought in, say, three times as much as anyone else.

Make sure your selection process is slick and identifies what you need it to. I have never found it helpful to ask a rookie to prepare a presentation on your industry and where the opportunity is. All that seems to assess is their internet search skills.

What I have found helpful, however, is the use of psychometric questionnaires. They give me and the candidate comfort that, on the balance of probabilities, this is going to work out. Actually, I think it's negligent to hire people if you don't have that.

I have used a combination of aptitude and ability tests. The first, remember, identifies *behavioural preferences*. The second one I chose measured someone's fluid intelligence at speed. To me, a very highly driven person with a low level of fluid intelligence is like a bull in a china shop. That person doesn't listen to feedback or adjust their approach. They are impervious to coaching and those with a low level of fluid intelligence will rapidly reach the low peak of their potential.

Please don't think you can use exam results as a substitute for a test of fluid intelligence. I have interviewed people who have the same degree, are awarded the same class, from the same university. But one of them has slaved away diligently in the library for 3 years, while the other has pulled some all-nighters to get their essay in, joined lots of groups and activities, done some paid work and broadened their horizons. I know which one I'd hire. Every time.

Some of the larger organisations I have worked with have enough historical data from tests, allowing us to analyse and find which profiles are most likely to be successful. Interestingly, the old, "lazy Z" profile (please Google it) is less useful in a more mature organisation which requires *some* orientation towards following processes.

So, you have understood what your culture is and how it might change.

We have discussed the need to develop yourself. And the need to hire on the right factors, and how that might change.

Now let's discuss how learning and development is an intrinsic part of this mix.

Some years ago, I was engaged by a RBL, D, who had plateaued at 40 staff.

His actual profitability, though, had plummeted. After achieving good levels of profitability by hiring colleagues from his former employer (who had proven BD skills and a similar understanding of culture) he embarked on a big expansion plan.

Over the course of two years, the business had expanded from 12 to 40 staff. But they had hired nearly 130 in that period.

Now, there were a number of things contributing to this. First, the business was being driven by growth at any cost. They often hired people they were doubtful about.

Second, they had very little understanding of management. There were dozens of KPIs, but no real attention to those which really mattered. The entire focus was on quantity, not quality or direction. They ended people's probation three months after start if they had billed anything, but had no other means of knowing if they were on track.

"But I *have* invested in training," D told me. He certainly had. He had sent people on lots of external, open courses, bought stacks of videos and more recently had employed a Master Practitioner in Neuro-Linguistic Programming.

With exactly zero recruitment experience.

Of the staff he had added, nearly all were underperforming seriously. All that "investment" was just cost.

Now, here's the thing. **He didn't know what they were being taught. And there was no implementation plan for that learning.**

I am proud to report that after four months, the changes I made led to a tripling of their average billings. It was a lot of hard work and I had the support of some excellent coaches that I hired.

First, I listened to what they were doing and looked at the outcomes. I was able to use my experience to identify some of the important skills, techniques and tools they didn't have.

Secondly, I agreed on a plan for what we were trying to achieve. I got the management team to accept that what I was proposing to implement was likely to achieve what they were looking for. This is a big step for many RBLs who think of L&D as a diversionary activity (being told entertaining anecdotes) or a "pick-me-up" or a buffet of ideas and suggestions from which they can take their pick.

I introduced them to Kirkpatrick's 5 levels of evaluation:

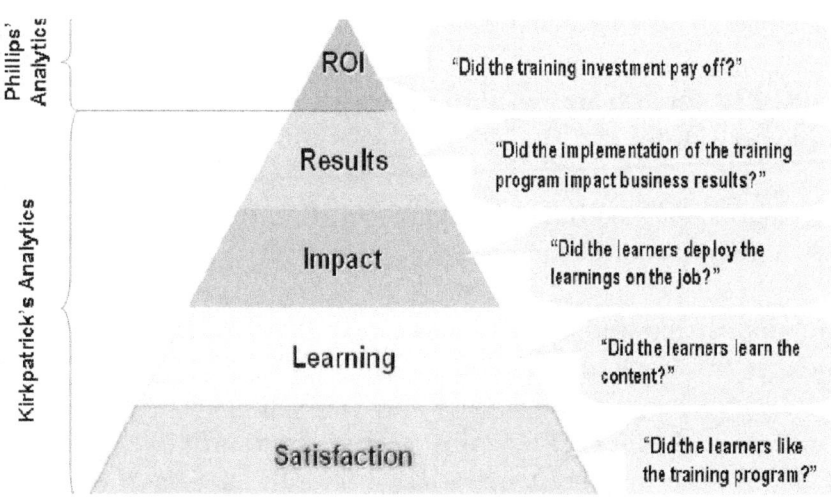

(I have a postgraduate diploma in L&D, so here's the technical bit).

We identified that most external trainers only measure the most basic level - satisfaction. This is done by issuing "happy sheets" which might as well ask, "did you have a laugh? Were the sandwiches nice?" for all they tell you about effectiveness.

The second level of evaluation is learning. How much has been understood and committed to memory? I agreed on a "test" for the trainees that their managers could implement. Just knowing there would be a test definitely made people pay more attention, by the way, especially if they had worked in the "L&D as buffet" environment before.

Then we agreed on some interim measures of impact. Fees would not come instantaneously, but we benchmarked current levels of new jobs registered and interviews arranged, so we could see that things were on track to improve.

Obviously, we looked at results, finally, in terms of billing increases. But there was also a significant impact on staff attrition. And the ROI on profit, therefore, ran into many multiples.

It wasn't only about training content. It was about having a proper plan for implementation.

Frankly, some really good RBLs just can't justify this sort of spend when they are starting up. They have to take advantage of external courses.

But the most successful ones do make sure they understand the content and have an implementation plan.

They understand that real learning needs a structure like this. And don't be shy. If you want to create lasting change through L&D, you'll need to create usable templates, acronyms and visual reminders. You may need to change your KPIs, incentives and even your CRM.

Don't bank on "practice makes perfect". It doesn't. But it does tend to make permanent. So, if your people are just repeating/practising mediocre recruitment, it will become "the way we do things around here".

In other words, great L&D lifts a culture of excellence if you have hired coachable people.

Along the way, I have sometimes had to delegate L&D to a dedicated L&D manager so I could cover all the other aspects of the business. I'm lucky that I have been able to hire some great people. But a couple of notes:

It makes sense to keep a L&D person close to actual results. I have created bonus schemes for them based on business objectives and measurable in P&L terms, or percentage increases in certain KPIs.

Have someone else check what actual learning is happening, for example by getting line managers to assess it against a set of objective criteria, or "milestones".

Otherwise, you run the risk of the L&D Manager "going rogue", by which I mean just "entertaining" staff with the latest theories and YouTube clips.

Once you have really good training in place for new starters, you will want to look at continuing to develop people further. It's one of the frequent contributors to staff attrition after probation that people's initial enthusiasm wanes, their skills are at a level of basic competence, but they aren't seeing the escalation of results (and reward) they had been led to expect.

Remember, practice does *not* make perfect.

Let's move on to management development.

When you start to build a management team, you will probably fall into the trap of promoting your biggest billers. There's been so much written and shared about this that I'm not going to repeat it here. I could tell you of many, many RBLs who have done this and regretted it.

The point I do want to make concerns developing managers. If your business is going to have capital value, it needs to be able to run without you. That's why this is so important.

I worked with F for three years. He was not the original owner of the business but had done a fine job of hiring good people, skilling them up and building a great reputation in the market. He understood the need for structure and the right incentives and was also a great all-rounder with a good handle on finance, marketing and tech.

Intending to create a clear career path for them, we worked on a career planner that integrated well with training and KPIs.

But F went further and made people managers to keep momentum in their careers. He didn't clarify what being a manager in that business required.

So he ended up with a business in which there was just 1.2 other staff for each "manager". It was costing him money, but he was still doing all the work.

He couldn't understand why his managers weren't picking up on underperformance. Or noticing serious conduct issues.

In the end, we used the same approach as we had to train the recruiters.

First, we clarified what good looked like. All the way down to what meetings we expected them to have and how frequently. What management information they should review and when. We also updated a number of his staff policies to give managers a bit of clarity, and in reality, a bit of clout.

Then we trained them to do all these things well.

And F made sure that managers' rewards reflected good management, not just good billing. And, after a while, F had to have a "difficult conversation" with a few of them. It was a relief all around, it turns out.

It is often said that being a billing manager is the hardest job in recruitment. I don't think I agree.

I think it's usually your *first* management job. And if no one tells you how to do it, it's going to be hard for sure.

In summary:
- **Know what characteristics indicate likely success**
- **Hire with care**
- **Clarify expectations and teach people how**
- **Reinforce learning with templates, reminders, incentives**
- **Measure ROI**
- **Culture may change, but it is led by you**

CHAPTER SIX

BEHAVIOUR 5: THE AGILITY
OF OPTIMISM

Kodak. Nokia, Xerox. Blockbuster. All businesses that are widely understood to have failed after occupying a market-leading position, because they did not innovate.

Let me give you an alternative list. FTX, WeWork, Segway, Boo.com. All businesses that managed to get an extraordinary amount of investment before working out their business model.

FTX was a cryptocurrency exchange business run by Sam Bankman-Fried. When his multi-million dollar fortune and business empire collapsed, he admitted that he ran this business based on nothing but reckless market assumptions and a hope that his run of luck would continue.

Most of the investors in these businesses knew the valuations they were being given didn't make sense, but no one wanted to be first to call out the "emperor's new clothes". They hoped that if they could keep the momentum going through brand marketing and spending, they could squeeze in an IPO and cash out. The founders were not in it for social revolution. Just to make a fortune.

So, what has that got to do with recruitment, and you as a RBL? Well, I have consistently observed that **most people who choose to start a recruitment business are optimists.** With a capital O.

But the most successful RBLs take it one step further. **That optimism allows them and their businesses to be agile, even as they reach considerable scale. They keep sense-checking.**

I tend to think that you *have* to be an optimist to start a new business. It's written into the person specification for a founder. Statistically, you are probably going to fail.

Data from the US Bureau of Labor Statistics show that approximately 20% of new businesses fail during the first two years of being open, 45% during the first five years, and 65% during the first 10 years. In the UK, it's even grimmer. The Telegraph reported that 20% of start-ups fail in their first year of business, and 60% won't make it past 3 years of trading.

And yet 6000 new recruitment businesses were started in the UK in 2021 alone. Optimism bias is essential to progress. Without it, records would not be broken, innovations created, and diseases eliminated.

According to an American study, 65% of people believe they have above-average intelligence (*source: https://www.ncbi.nlm.nih.gov/*). We also tend to believe that we will live longer than data suggests, flourish where others have failed, and believe that our children will be more talented and cleverer than average.

So, optimism bias is not unique to successful RBLs, it's in those that do much less well too. It is the *combination* of optimism with all the other behaviours in this book that, I suggest, gives the successful RBLs their Agility.

Allow me to introduce you to two business partners, N and O. They had established a business in temporary logistics recruitment, having come from the industry themselves.

From the outside, recruitment looked simple. They were very confident that they could improve on what most recruiters appeared to do (just finding CVs, wasn't it?) and trade with their contacts in the sector using their market knowledge. Their market had become dominated by master service providers, which paid them low margins but sent them plenty of requirements to keep them busy.

At the point I met them, two years on, the business had not delivered in the way they had expected. There was a lot that was wrong with it (cash flow, debt collection, no systematic business development, low-skilled recruiters, poor quality data, and that's just for starters). Fundamentally, they were resourcers and order-takers.

(By the way, they are far from alone in this. I observe across all sectors a "generation" of so-called recruitment consultants who have only really known a market in which employer demand is high and there are lots of jobs to fill. Faced with a scenario where they have to talk business with a client who doesn't have a job, they are stumped. But I digress. We'll talk more about that in the last chapter, "Make a Plan".)

N was absolutely clear that they should "stick to the knitting". By shaving off some costs and waiting for demand to pick up again, he was optimistic that they could keep going.

O was also optimistic. But he was optimistic because he wanted to redirect their efforts into permanent recruitment which would bring much-needed cashflow. Luckily, most of their agreements with the master service providers (recruitment processing outsourcing (RPO) companies) didn't preclude this. Therefore they could do it, but it would require them to become prospectors and business developers, to deal with more senior-level staff than they had previously, and to learn to negotiate and source candidates more creatively.

Now, O had put his periscope up and looked at data in the market. He had also kept in mind the "Why" of the business (although they hadn't really articulated it) which was to provide rapid access to talent that logistics clients can't find themselves. What they needed was a plan to do that, because they didn't have data to work with, skills or a candidate database.

As resources were limited (O and one other recruiter to develop the permanent business), we needed to be very focused. We worked up a very challenging plan to identify and speak to a specific number of hiring managers in one area only and to break into the market by offering a "fixed price model" rather than the percentage of salary that is traditional.

We hit on this offer, again, because when you try to break into a new market, your biggest enemy is the status quo.

When you ask clients to use you for the first time, it's not risk-free for them, even if it is on a "payment on results" basis. They risk you not coming through for them, and the waste of time on briefing you, reviewing your candidates, etc. But they also risk having a key role remain unfilled. And that might mean that they lose a client of theirs, can't bid for a contract, miss a key piece of compliance, or continue to pile more pressure on the rest of the team.

In turn, that means that they suffer personal and reputational risk. Indeed, when managers routinely make poor buying decisions, waste business time or can't fill jobs, it can be career-limiting.

But we needed something that O could sell with conviction. His message to hiring managers was clear - if you think that recruiters seek to inflate pay to inflate their fees, use us. We won't do any less work on your vacancy.

Yes, O had to work on his business development skills and needed some support. But in this case, it did work. There was a pleasant bonus in that he was able to persuade a few employers to use him exclusively because it was a known, budget-able price per hire.

We decided to buy in some data to create a database quickly for direct marketing purposes. But from the outset, the permanent side of the business kept good quality data on all the jobs, clients and candidates they contacted, so their networks grew.

This is Ansoff's matrix:

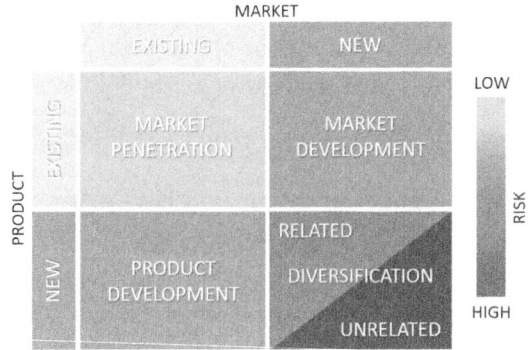

It's a graphic which illustrates the opportunities for businesses to develop.

So, if you currently recruit accountants for businesses in Birmingham, then option 1 is to recruit more accountants for those clients (top left).

Option 2 is to recruit other types of staff or supply other services to the same clients - like temporary staff (bottom left).

Option 3 is to sell to new clients, for example in London, OR the public sector (top right).

Option 4 is to diversify - sell new products to new clients, like moving into healthcare staffing. Or training accounts staff (bottom right). That requires the most investment.

The most successful RBLs I know are always alert to opportunity.

Like E, who saw Covid as an opportunity to develop his permanent recruitment business into retained search. Later, he offered recruitment and retention training to clients. And he went on the front foot with IR35 to demonstrate compliance and how using his business would protect clients from HMRC investigation.

The most successful RBLs see the opportunity in change. And adopt a growth mindset.

In case you aren't familiar with the term, someone with a growth mindset views intelligence, abilities, and talents as learnable and capable of improvement through effort.

On the other hand, someone with a fixed mindset views those same traits as inherently stable and unchangeable over time.

For example, as an aspiring entrepreneur, you need basic finance skills to create a budget and interpret your accounts. With a fixed mindset, you may think, "I've never been good at maths, let alone financial statements. I'm not cut out to run my own business."

Now imagine you approach the situation with a growth mindset. You might think, "I don't have a background in finance, but I can learn and practise those skills until I feel capable".

So the keywords to add to your "self-talk" are "yet" and "and". Instead of "I can't do that", think, "I can't do that yet, but I will find someone to teach me, and practise".

When I think about how the industry responded to Covid, many people I know deserve congratulations on how quickly they adapted. The thing is the technologies that enabled that adaptation had been available for nearly a decade.

Let's be honest. Most businesses' digital strategy was not driven by the CTO or the CEO. It was driven by a virus.

I'd like to give you an example of Agility on an even bigger scale. There is more detail on the "How to" in my e-book, Revolutionary Recruitment, which is available for free via my website if you are interested.

Years ago, Boots (a pharmacy chain) was rapidly losing market share. Supermarkets were now allowed to sell a huge chunk of the stock that previously had to be sold by a pharmacist, like paracetamol and anti-histamines.

The CEO at the time saw a huge stock of retail space that was becoming less profitable (retailers measure their profit by sales per square metre of sales floor space). That CEO wanted to find new ways to trade on their brand value, among the most trusted brands in Britain at the time. So, they set up Opticians. Dentists were to follow.

By the time I came in contact with the executive team appointed to do this (just a handful of people at this stage), they were able to give me a clear idea of the challenges:

- Dentists were traditionally self-employed and well-rewarded
- Shop space had to be fitted out, staffed and operational in a very tight turnaround schedule
- To build the brand, dentists had to display certain standards and behaviours
- There was a finite budget for staffing
- Boots did not have staff to dedicate to this

I had never been involved in healthcare or dentistry recruitment at that time. If I'm honest, I had never sold or delivered a project of that size before. But (with the support of an excellent delivery team) I designed a solution that was based on a strong advertising campaign, a standardised telephone screening process and assessment centres. The contract was negotiated via three days of intense discussions with Boots' procurement team. It was worth about £12 million in 2001.

So, a bit of a game-changer. And I have gone on to, personally, create very successful statement of works businesses in three different companies.

I met P when she was running a very small, specialist business focused on a niche engineering market. She had herself worked as an engineer and had built a business based on her own remarkable understanding and hard work.

P had done business with some of the biggest names on the planet. With just two staff. But she found it difficult to attract staff and wanted to establish a more sustainable income.

So, having established a contract team, she started to see bigger possibilities. Because she understood engineering, she was able to get access to engineering entrepreneurs, even before they got funding, and wanted to take a bigger offer to them. That offer was to provide a whole talent service - from defining the employer brand using her expertise, to crafting a targeted attraction campaign, to delivering onboarding and some induction processes.

Here's the thing. She was taking this offer to people before they even knew what they wanted, or what was possible. The most successful

RBLs don't wait for clients to come to them with a specification for a service like this.

As Henry T. Ford is widely quoted as saying; "If I'd asked my customers what they wanted, they would have said faster horses".

Another client, L, was involved in a sales recruitment business which lacked differentiation or a business plan. They were regularly struggling with clients who didn't pay, or flaky candidates, and wanted to move to more strategic roles. As part of this change, I showed them how to sell retainers and we defined a much more robust selection process that they could take to market. But clients were still having to take it on trust that L would deliver.

L took the best of the search methodology and created a platform that made the search process visible. It allowed his clients to see video presentations of the candidates, their CVs, references and psychometric profiles, as well as their answers to some scenarios or competency-based questions, in one place. This enabled the team to show a visible "product" for the search process to prospective clients and it really took off, internationally.

It was so successful that L was able to license it to many other recruiters. You may even have met him or used the product.

You will have spotted that a RBL can't come up with agile approaches like this unless they have feelers in the client and candidate communities. And, yes, a growth mindset.

This is diversification, but it's not ignoring your "Why".

Customers change. You may be in a market in which RPOs and frameworks are being widely adopted by employers. You can decide to work with that but get more efficient in your delivery mechanisms because your margins are likely to get considerably smaller. Or you can decide not to buy in and try to work "off framework". But if you do, you will need to have better relationships, harder-to-find candidates and speedy processes.

When their traditional market starts changing, many recruiters go into denial (like N in the earlier example). I remember all the way back to my time at Robert Half International (a massive financial recruiter, headquartered in the US), in the 1980s and 1990s. "*Never* deal with HR" was the message from the US.

The UK business was not in the same market-dominant position that the US business enjoyed. And HR was starting to become a powerful force (although not nearly as powerful as it is now).

(I don't have any data for this, but employment law and protections remain comparatively limited in the US, so it may be that HR in the UK was more influential than in the US at the time).

Anyway, Robert Half US had enjoyed great success dealing directly with hiring managers. And they were, at that time, in denial.

Are you familiar with the Grief Cycle described by Elisabeth Kubler Ross? It describes the stages of grief (bereavement, but people do go through something like that when they lose what is familiar - in this case, their market).

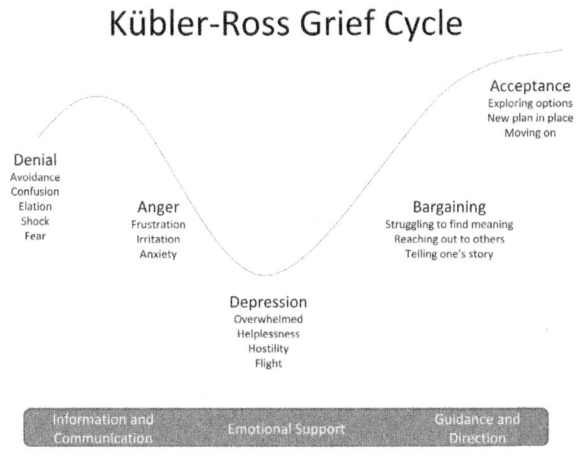

Kübler-Ross Grief Cycle

I've been working in the recruitment industry for so long that I've seen this phenomenon quite a few times.

People predicted the end of days when online job boards were invented. They said that employment law, including the Equality Act, would destroy employers' ability to select effective staff.

Then the Working Time Regulation and Minimum Wage Legislation were going to make small recruitment businesses impossible to run. The Agency Workers Act was going to bring about the end of the temporary staffing industry. Then it was IR35, and then the changes in liability under IR35.

So, the denial phase is a given. **But optimistic, agile recruitment business leaders are alert to change and see opportunity.**

In a few cases, they are so "up for it" that they have already got to "acceptance" when their team are still in "denial".

So, they have to become great change managers too. It is not enough to present your team with incontrovertible data. Or just to give them the "Braveheart speech" and tell them to get on with it.

For change to really stick, I've found that it needs more than the facts. Otherwise, nobody would smoke or become obese.

So in business, your team needs to **understand the need** for change, but also have **the will** to change. They need to **know how** to change and get **relevant training**. They need the **tools for change**, whether that be technical capabilities, data, or marketing collateral. **Reminders and prompts** (like templates) are also helpful.

Then they need to know that you will be **checking on progress**. Not necessarily big business wins, but midway checks, for example, that they have arranged meetings to present the new proposition.

And you will also need to look at **incentives**. Afterwards, you may have to consider **penalties**.

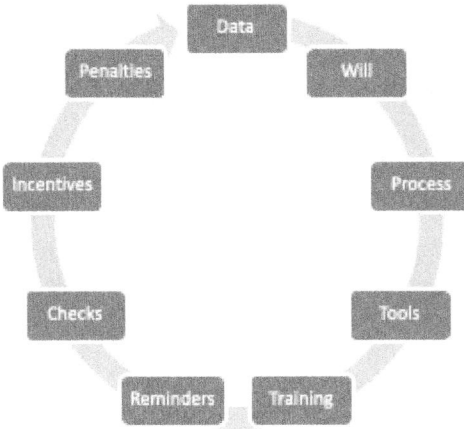

So, when O wanted to change the service that the business was offering, it didn't happen overnight. But our plan started with data and collateral, included training, and focused, in the short term, on client meetings and jobs registered, rather than invoiced revenues.

A note on resilience

I think that we have come a long way with our understanding of resilience in recent years. The emphasis on workplace wellbeing and mental health has contributed.

Resilience in successful RBLs is not stubbornness, in my opinion. It is the Agility of Optimism.

In summary:
- **Adopt a growth mindset**
- **Keep looking for opportunity**
- **Don't wait for clients to come to you**
- **Manage change within your organisation.**

CHAPTER SEVEN
BEHAVIOUR 6: ESTABLISHING STRONG ROOTS

Sometimes I get contacted by businesses that have "failed to launch". They find things aren't getting any easier and they suffer from never quite getting into top gear because of crises and staff turnover.

There is always something that can be done to improve the business. But sometimes the problem is so deep-rooted in the culture of the business that I have thought the owners might be better off terminating everyone and starting again. Some of them have said that to me.

Of course, the problem is that they need income. There are the livelihoods of their staff to consider and their families. The business has commitments in terms of supplier agreements, licences and so on.

Remember, your biggest enemy to scaling is when the status quo is generating a mediocre level of success.

I was fortunate, in my very early career, to be given a chance to start two companies, but with the safety net of working for Hays. The business could afford to invest in new markets and wait to convert profits. (They were ruthless about stopping or changing personnel if the new ventures didn't at least break even in a year. That's quite a good rule of thumb even now).

So, I appreciate I didn't have the pressure of trying to put food on the table. I can understand, however, how business owners get trapped by becoming hostage to one or two "big billers".

In the case of one business I advised, in oil and gas recruitment, they had one person (H) who routinely billed well. He had landed on a specialist niche in the market at a good time, and there was no doubt that he also had good recruitment skills. Having been headhunted from another agency, he was already on a high basic salary.

H told the owner, N, he needed new tools and licences to maintain this level of success. N duly supplied them and revenues continued to rise. In fact, H got so busy that he needed resourcers to use these tools and screen all the candidates that were now being generated.

Now, N was not stupid. He recognised that H was sitting on a potential goldmine and he wanted to maximise the revenues from it. So, he asked H to find another consultant - H went and headhunted a former colleague. Then H went back to N and demanded a pay increase to reflect his seniority relative to the newly-hired consultant.

N swallowed hard. He didn't want to upset his star biller, so he promised to review it. He ended up paying him a percentage of the new consultant's billings - double-dipping.

The new consultant did not set the roof alight with his success. H said he was a bit lazy, and didn't seem able to develop business. But N agreed to give it time.

What was actually going on? H had decided that any client he had ever made contact with was his. So, while he controlled which jobs the new consultant had to work, he also claimed the lion's share of the fee each time.

The new consultant spent a lot of time looking for leads but lost heart when he found H's initials next to everyone on the CRM.

Still, N didn't get under the bonnet as he didn't want to rock the boat. The profitability of the division was now less than when H worked alone. You guessed it

- eventually, H left and set up on his own, using every bit of the data he had gained at N's expense.

No matter how strong the pull is, do not be taken hostage by one or two big billers.

What N did next time (the market was quite prone to boom and bust, so he waited a bit) was establish clear and regular reviews of the pipeline with the consultant who remained, and when it was steady enough to hire another, *he* decided how the market should be split (by job function, as it happened). So the consultant who had stayed kept his client relationships, but between them, the two consultants generated more contacts and more leads.

N also insisted that everything went on the CRM.

No details on the CRM, no commission.

No report from a client meeting, no expenses.

But without the opportunity to start again, I doubt N would ever have escaped being in thrall to his biggest biller.

Closely linked to this, I want to discuss overpaying. I touched on this in earlier chapters.

If your potential new hire in your early growth phase is only interested in what they can take from the business, step away.

No matter where you are on your path, as previously discussed, you should look to build networks for possible future hires. But some people in the industry take a "headhunt approach" as permission to put outrageous demands on the table.

They want to work from home. They want very high basic salaries. They want super-bonuses. They want equity.

Nothing wrong with a bit of ambition. But what they aren't interested in (other than the title) is managing. No, their aim is *not* to help you build a robust business. It's to maximise their own profitability, and that's all. (If I sound bitter, it's because I experienced this a long time ago).

Many of the RBLs I meet are quite clued up about exit routes. They want to set up an Enterprise Management Scheme (EMI) scheme really early (in my view it's usually too early if you have less than £500,000 earnings before tax and interest) in order to keep a sense of momentum and tie in great people.

If you go at this too early, the business isn't really worth very much. So, you hand out quite large percentages of equity to have the "golden handcuffs" impact.

And then you begin to realise the limitations of the people you have given it to. Sometimes, their experience may even be confined to working for you, so they are not even adding anything to the business. But they are getting handsomely rewarded, *and* they have shares.

So my advice is to hang on. **Build a management infrastructure first, and reward those key personnel with growth shares or options**. Your biggest billers are already getting rewarded through your commission scheme.

I know a few people who have fallen into this trap. G had established her own IT consultancy, with four consultants and one marketing administrator when she decided to announce a share scheme. She then gave 5% of the business to each of them and an additional 5% to her accountant and her mentor, both of whom rapidly took their feet off the gas.

The young consultants just took the equity without understanding what it meant. **It did not influence their behaviour one bit.** They carried on demanding basic pay rises and extra incentives. **Don't be that person.**

In chapter 4, under the heading, "Engagement" I mentioned a RBL who had tried to copy every benefit that every competitor was offering.

This is an inflationary race and we have probably all seen evidence of it.

It will end up screwing your pay-out ratio and starving the business of investment (not to mention starving you as the leader).

So, I urge you to focus on what your employer brand is. You cannot be all things to all people. At the listed companies I have worked at, their brand was about reputation, established networks and incoming business. The consultants were well-supported by big brand marketing spend and training.

They did not pay the highest commission. In fact, they paid low basic salaries as well (I recall that my basic salary was just £3500 when I joined one in 1985 and an online inflation calculator tells me that's about £10,200 now). But decent recruiters earned plenty. I was in the higher rate tax band in my first twelve months.

Independent businesses need to offer something different to attract motivated people. I've worked with independent businesses who have been "employers of choice" despite a long-hours culture, or in another case, working in frankly horrible offices.

It's like supermarkets. If you think your market is competitive, it has nothing on the UK grocery market. Margins are tight, competition is fierce and customers are flighty. Look at the market share achieved by Aldi (now fourth biggest) in record time against the behemoths with a history of more than 100 years.

So, supermarkets are constantly evolving their brands. Where the discounters, Aldi and Lidl, sell on price, Tesco sells on range and Waitrose sells on quality and innovation. People choose their store less by proximity (especially since so much shopping is now done online) and more by brand message.

Know your employer brand. Attract people who respond to that.

And decide on a reward system that rewards the behaviours you want.

Several people I know, on learning that I was writing this book, asked me if I was going to include "the perfect commission scheme". Sorry to disappoint.

But here are the factors you should consider:

- Are you permanent recruitment led? Or temporary/contract? You need incentives to grow a temp desk, but the end returns will be greater. You don't have to pay out the same percentage of net fee income.
- What is the average size of the fee, and frequency of billing? If it's a business that relies on fewer, bigger fees you will need to consider how you reward consistency.
- What is the gap between boarding, invoicing and receiving fees? When will you pay the commission? Is there a significant drop-off between these stages?
- How much do your desks cost? That's a percentage of overheads, which you have almost certainly added to as you grow, including business support staff. You may well need to consider a threshold.
- Is your main business driver new business? Or account development? Reward what you want to achieve.
- Is the market candidate-driven, or jobs-led? Is there a meaningful teamwork element to success? Split fees accordingly.
- How well-established is the business or division?
- How often do you need to pay out commission? If it's a high-volume business, you probably want more frequent, smaller payouts.

Please don't fall into making your commission scheme contractual.

Yes, people need clarity and it must be written down. But you can revise a *policy* (no more than once a year maximum) to reflect market conditions.

And remember that if it is never revised you may have made it a de facto contractual right.

When I worked with P, an energy recruiter, I found he was tied into a contractual commission scheme because when he had made his first hire, he had asked a lawyer to prepare a contract for him. The lawyer assumed he had no policies, so put absolutely everything in the contract for that individual. And P had simply used the same one ever since.

As you can imagine, it was very difficult to unpick (although we could change the arrangement for future hires).

But P was trapped by the behaviours that the scheme encouraged, plus a mindset that commission was an extra profit share, while salary should be the vast majority of reward.

As you can imagine, this arrangement only worked one way. If performance dropped, the salary remained in place.

I said in the chapter "Iterative Improvement" that culture, hiring and L&D were all intertwined. I'd like to develop this further now.

"The culture of an organisation is determined by the worst level of behaviour that the leadership will tolerate".

If you want to grow from strong roots, **don't ever imagine that culture is something you can sort out later.**

You know, on that "magic day" when you've got plenty of money in the bank and everything is ticking over nicely. Because by then it will be too late. If that day ever comes.

I'm sure you know yourself of examples where damaging behaviours have been tolerated because it was the biggest biller, or "it was a one-off". Here are just some examples:

- Staff conducting multiple affairs at work, simultaneously
- Staff deciding to celebrate "directors' lunch" by taking drugs in the restaurant toilets, getting the whole group banned
- Staff getting uncontrollably intoxicated at client entertainment events and insulting client staff
- Staff "saving up" placements once they had reached an acceptable minimum each month, therefore keeping overall performance down
- Staff who collude with clients to discriminate unlawfully (ironically then complain about candidate shortages)
- Staff who don't bother to explain terms to clients, or even send them

If you tolerate this, you have established a culture that will simply encourage others to adjust their behaviour, or performance, to suit. Or leave.

Even if the team member's conduct is a total aberration, you need to use your disciplinary process. Promptly and proportionally.

That includes having a usable performance improvement process (PIP) in place.

Now, I would hazard a guess that most businesses are not doing this well. Why?

Because most RBLs carry baggage about PIPs. They think that someone who has had a bad month will come good and that invoking a PIP process will just depress them.

Because they think that a PIP is equivalent to terminating their employment, which they don't want to do.

Because they think the member of staff will get better if we give them time.

Because they don't want to cause unpleasantness.

Because they don't know how to do it.

Because they don't want to be seen to do it to this person when they didn't do it for another in similar circumstances.

Because they have no idea how to improve performance.

Or because they are relying on an "off the shelf" disciplinary process based on conduct, and there is nothing wrong with the recruiter's conduct.

I'm going to come right out and say it. All of these excuses are just that.

They leave you open to claims of discrimination (no upper limit on fines, BTW) and unfair dismissal. They create a sense of unfairness or at least a damaging impression of what is acceptable performance.

But mainly because if you don't intervene and fix whatever is damaging the recruiter's performance, it is a huge opportunity missed. An opportunity to help that person quickly.

Whether they need better organisation, or to revisit training, or better direction of their efforts, or some other support, they will be really appreciative of prompt and proportional help.

If you do it well.

Just shouting at them to make more calls, or work harder is not good enough. You (or their line manager) need to sit with them at their desk to work out a plan.

Because nobody comes to work intending to do a bad job.

I've seen many people have a PIP and then go on to perform as a star recruiter, manager or even director of a business. They are my poster children for this process.

My advice on PIPs: Choose your "triggers" carefully. Diagnose carefully. Implement universally.

In the last section of this chapter, I'd like to talk to you about a business that had grown substantially when I got involved. The founders were great salespeople and managers and had grown the business to this point by creating healthy competition for candidates and jobs between their team members. They had hundreds of contractors on assignment.

But by the time they had reached 30 consultants, the scrapping over candidates wasn't really working anymore. No one was incentivised to record data about them on the CRM.

No one maintained contact with candidates who were on assignment, especially if they were on assignment through another agency. They were too busy chasing new business.

Consequently, candidates were receiving multiple calls, texts and emails from different staff at this agency. The result was that they had little faith that the agency was looking out for them. They got fed up with the repeated questions and lack of recording of what they had said.

So we agreed to change the system, even though the business was doing well. There was a strong gravitational pull against change, and (as you can imagine) the team saw it only in terms of loss. When they were asked to limit their candidates to a maximum of 100 each, and take really good care of them, it seemed to be limiting their reach.

But that process led to substantially improved redeployment of their workers because they knew them well and could plan for finding their next assignment.

It meant that the consultants cultivated the best contractors, not those who were unreliable or had poor references.

And they were better positioned to get recommendations, referrals and market intelligence from their contractors.

The organisation more than doubled its staff in a quarter of the time after that. They had put the plug in the proverbial bath, rather than just running more water.

In another case, a business had grown over a long period to a multi-branch operation. The directors prided themselves on the quality of their highly consultative service. **But their clients kept using other agencies. Why?**

The staff had assumed that their service would speak for itself. Having experienced the difference, clients would use them again and recommend them. In some cases, they did. But not nearly enough.

So, they kept looking for new business. Which, as we know, is expensive and challenging. Work never seemed to get any easier and that had an impact on staff turnover.

It only turned around when we brought in an account development plan.

It started with every client we had worked with in the last 12 months, and included mapping the organisation, getting a testimonial and arranging a meeting. We later extended an amended version to every client who had registered a job that we had *not* filled.

Yes, if you are starting up your business you have to start somewhere.

But don't just focus on filling jobs. There is so much more to recruitment than that.

In summary:
- **Don't be taken hostage**
- **Reward loyal managers**

- **Actively support your culture**
- **Manage performance**
- **Don't just fill jobs**

CHAPTER EIGHT
BEHAVIOUR 7: MAKE A PLAN

Proper implementation beats ideas.

Congratulations! You're still reading, and that tells me you have staying power. With a bit of luck, you've made some notes about things you want to change or review in your business.

But here's the thing. On the balance of probabilities, you probably won't action them.

Why? Our old friend, the status quo, or "business gravitational pull".

You know how when you've been to a conference, or on a course, you come back to your desk bristling with inspiration? But there are just a few urgent emails that need dealing with before you start on that.

And then some of the notes you've taken need to be reorganised. This is a slightly bigger project than you thought. It needs to wait for the "magic day" when your diary has some great big empty space in it.

And by the time you get to those notes, they no longer seem quite as relevant as they did at the time. In fact, you can't even remember what some of them mean.

We've all been there. Take E, a really sociable lady who had developed a career in a niche area of life sciences. She had a network that spanned the globe. In her mid-life, she decided to establish a recruitment agency based on those contacts. She loved the sociable nature of working in recruitment as opposed to in a lab.

But after some initial success, her business had shrunk back to very little. Some of her contacts had retired or moved on. And she had no plan for business development. Now that her children had left home, she really wanted (and needed) to build the business.

One of the first things we tackled was the lack of any brand differentiation (remember "Start with the Why?") and that, in turn, made her shy about contacting anyone new. As she only had one member of staff at the time, who was relatively inexperienced, we kept it simple. To start, she was going to follow up on all of her old placements, and aim to get one client lead from each.

This was one of a number of actions that I had detailed in the minutes. Each action had a "by when?" And "by who?" written next to it.

But when I returned to see her, it was clear that E had not made the progress I'd hoped.

Why? Too busy. Urgent matters. I introduced her to the urgent/important matrix. Just in case you haven't seen it:

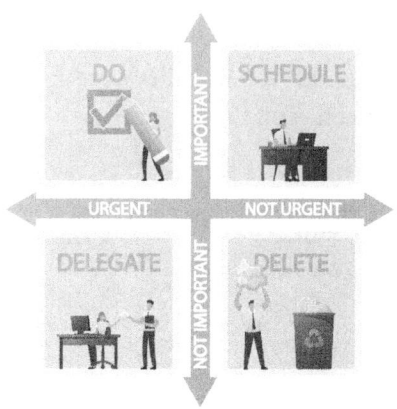

E nodded enthusiastically. She understood the theory, but in practice, not so much. When we looked at how she was spending her day, it seemed to be dictated by what popped into her inbox or by dealing with queries from her employee.

And *everything*, always, seemed urgent.

Much later, another client put this syndrome in a really memorable way. He said, **"no 'ing' words allowed"**.

As he pointed out in staff reviews, his team were clearly *not* "doing it now", whatever the action was that they had promised to implement. They were sitting with him in a review meeting and hadn't made progress. So, the use of the present participle ("ing words") wasn't even appropriate.

Back to E. Next time I saw her, she had made some progress but she seemed stressed. Why?

Because while she was now making those calls daily, *she hadn't stopped doing anything else.*

So, here are the first three lessons in implementation:

1. Write down your commitments. Diarise "by when" and make sure you know who is responsible.

2. Make time for what's truly important, not just what's urgent. The *important* things are your long-term goals, such as profit and internal hiring. The *urgent* things are, very often, to do with other people's agendas.

3. Recognise that, in order to do something new, **you will have to stop doing something else**.

Now, E's problems were relatively easy to solve because she ran a very small business (I'm pleased to say it's bigger now). The useful bi-product of this lesson was that she set a far better example for her staff, and it made it easier to manage them.

Change is a much more complex beast in a larger organisation.

Ideas are cheap. Good implementation is priceless.

I worked with two business partners, X and Y. (Yes, I really am running out of letters now. Thank goodness it's the last chapter.) They were both inspirational leaders. And they invited me to work with them because of my wider experience. They wanted to see what else could be done with the business to grow it. (You know who you are, guys!).

I had masses of plans. A statement of works business. Changes to processes. Turning around one team. Developing the management team. Creating a world-class L&D programme.

One of the things they were particularly good at, funnily enough, was telling me to slow down. As they put it, "you haven't dropped a ball. You've put it down in the corner to pick up later."

Points four and five:

4. Lasting change always takes longer and involves more resources than you think.
5. It will get harder as your organisation gets bigger.

So, if you're determined to grow your business, *you're going to need to be a change manager.* Particularly in a VUCA environment (please google it).

Let's think about a scenario we can all recognise. Let's say your business environment has become more difficult. There is downward pressure on fees, and you are working more jobs for less profit. As a RBL, along with your senior leadership team, you need to plan a route to keep your business on track for profitable growth.

First, **define your aims.**

Is your aim to manage for short-term profit? Or is it to find more jobs? Or to increase average fees?

It's important to get this right. Framing the aims carefully will make a big difference. Just think how different the courses of action would be for just the three different aims mentioned above.

I have observed, when coaching RBLs, that they are often too close to the problem to be sure that they have framed it correctly.

An example: The director of a business with 50 employees was experiencing frustration because so much of his time was spent helping less experienced staff do intelligent Boolean searches for specific candidates in their IT business.

It kept coming back to the director, in part because of his technical knowledge and in part because he was an active guy who really wanted to be of practical help. But he didn't have time to work on some of his bigger projects to improve the business.

He had framed his aim like this: how can I reduce the time spent?

I saw the problem differently. *Why* did these people continue to need his help years into their careers?

When we looked at it this way, it became clear that change was needed in the training they received and the way they were managed. Working with his L&D manager, he created a module on searching that she could teach, a library of saved searches, and tools for their managers to check progress.

The problem was not completely resolved, but over time people went to these resources first. And the managers' roles developed too.

Next, **look to external data**. This is easier if you service the public sector. However, organisations like the REC and your sector's professional bodies provide great data. Just beware of "trend reports" from organisations with a vested interest. **Do not rely on your gut, or "lived experience".**

Here's an example: I've previously been in the position of working with two companies which, coincidentally had small teams in the same market.

One was really succeeding. The RBLs at the other told me that there was no market - based on what their consultants were telling them. The main difference was their people, and the quantity, quality and direction of their business development efforts. A bit of competitor analysis can be very useful here. Check out their accounts as well as their LinkedIn page, though.

So, after taking soundings, you re-frame the issue, and the aim of your change project is agreed. In this example, you agree *to reposition your business in its current market by bringing in higher average fees through working more senior roles.*

The leadership team has checked that there is less pressure on fees where clients can see the strategic importance of the hire. Based on the data, you know that most senior candidates will be less flaky (lower drop-out rates) and easier to identify.

There are probably a dozen different approaches that could increase your profits. You could dismiss all your trainees. You could re-engineer and focus on volume recruitment through master service providers. But you've picked one.

This is why I'm not a subscriber to another much-repeated "truth". Often referred to as marginal gains, it's the idea that it is easier to improve 100 things by 1% than improve a couple of things significantly.

Maybe that works with individual recruiters. But by the time you're running a substantial business, that approach simply leads to confusion and change fatigue.

Next, you need a plan.

Consider what tools and training will be required. What information does the team need? And how exactly do you expect them to act differently?

Remember your changes may have knock-on effects. For example, your marketing and advertising will need to change, to focus on more senior roles.

Remember that people will have to stop doing something in order to do this. That's hard. You may need to give them a set of criteria to assess incoming vacancies (e.g. if the salary or fee percentage is below a certain level, or if it's impossible to get a proper brief from the hiring manager and there's no commitment from them).

Staff need reassurance that they can walk away. You know that saying: "how can you discover new lands if you can never lose sight of the shore?" It's an illusion that those low-level instructions are better than nothing. That is not a real binary choice. The real choice is to spend your valuable time building a profitable senior business or keep spending time working uncommitted jobs for lower fees.

I expect that's not news to you as a recruiter. But as a recruitment business leader, it's important. Don't be one of those leaders who constantly piles new actions, more KPIs and additional initiatives on your people without ever taking anything away.

Before you communicate the plan, you will also want to **benchmark current performance**. Let's say your average fee is currently £10,000. You decide that you will regard this change as successful when the average fee has increased by 10%, without making fewer placements (by the way, apply this same benchmarking before you bring in new L&D initiatives, otherwise, you can't possibly measure ROI - see chapter "Iterative Improvement").

Now, that is not going to happen overnight. It will involve renegotiating terms with some clients. Training staff. Getting referrals to more senior decision-makers. Changing website content, perhaps, and reposting adverts. All while keeping the money rolling in.

And you can't make this change at the expense of everything else, or you will end up in a worse position. It is important to **consider this change with a balanced scorecard in mind**.

Your agile mind will grasp this concept pretty quickly. Under "processes" you might ask yourself, "what information do we need to record? What new checks will we need? How will team leaders check up on progress?"

Under customer experience, you might measure customer satisfaction using net promoter scoring, or collecting testimonials. We don't want an initiative in one area to be detrimental to another area.

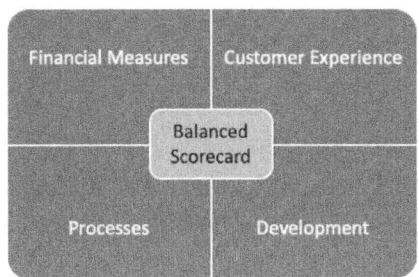

This is now looking more like a six-month change project than a six-day one.

So you need milestones. You probably won't be able to see the impact on your P&L quickly, and that's why lots of RBLs lose heart. Thinking it's not working, and everyone is complaining about the change, they give up.

For our project example, you might agree on milestones like X number of jobs at above Y salary taken by month three. You might want to have seen a certain number of final interviews arranged (associated with a fee of £X or more) by month five.

Each milestone will show you that you are on track. And should be a cause for celebration.

But let's say that the purpose of the change has got lost in its execution. You notice that, while your first milestone has been met, actual total gross profit is flatlining. Don't panic. You are just in the dip.

The dip is the part of change where it turns out to be harder and slower than you thought. Initial enthusiasm has been replaced by gritted teeth or even cynicism about the change. Keep reminding your team of the purpose and how it will benefit them.

You have to go from the comfort zone through the discomfort zone to reach the learning zone. And on the other side of that is the growth zone.

If there isn't sponsorship of the change at the highest level, it will fall apart. I've often seen boards agree that they need to make a change, but then wash their hands and "delegate" the project to someone who appears to have spare capacity. But that person has no authority in the business (diversity and inclusion is a classic casualty, delegated to a HR Officer and so "orphaned").

The sponsor has to have the power to allocate resources, manage objections and resolve competing demands. The sponsor is the RBL who reminds people of the purpose and checks on the milestones. They may design incentives, if necessary. Much later on, they may even have to design penalties for those who don't change.

Lastly, with bigger organisations and change projects, I have always found it helpful to **give people notice.** This allows time for consideration, questions and more detail to be documented.

Don't just try to *slide* into change without people noticing. The laws of nature are against you.

I want to say that it's a key part of being a successful RBL to consider what change will serve you and to manage that change. But not all changes have to be total business re-engineering along the lines of Facebook/Meta.

Just make plans before you start new things. Implementation beats ideas.

If you want to grow, have a sensible budget and a hiring plan (prioritised). Identify where the new business will come from. Schedule time to do the actions.

And remember, nothing changes until *you* change.

In summary:
- **Write down agreed actions**
- **Understand important vs urgent**
- **Make space for change by removing something else**
- **Carefully frame the issue and your aims**
- **Allow sufficient time to see ROI**
- **Use external data**
- **Benchmark current performance to measure ROI**
- **Make a plan with realistic "progress milestones"**
- **Don't try to slide into change**

Conclusion

Thanks for reading all the way to the end. I hope it's been beneficial, and that you have taken some real learning away to action.

There are loads more I'd love to share with you, but that would have to be just for you.

I wish you well.

Acknowledgements

I'd like to sincerely thank my clients, past and present, who have trusted me with advising them and even taken my advice when I have ticked them off. I am full of admiration for what you do.

And to past employers, who have taught me a lot by observing them, my sincere appreciation.

I'm sorry that I can't mention everyone by name, but if you think you recognise yourself in these chapters, thank you.

I'd also like to thank Zoe Jephtha, my marketing support at Loaded Hype, who initially urged me to write this.

And Virpi at businessillustrator.com whose great images are included.

And especially, my family, most particularly Paul, who has had his ears chewed off more times than I can say, and still listens.

Printed in Great Britain
by Amazon

21088034R00058